Velocity

THE BEST OF
APPLES & SNAKES

Velocity

THE BEST OF
APPLES & SNAKES

EDITOR: MAJA PRAUSNITZ
ASSISTANT EDITOR: GRETCHEN LADISH
ASSOCIATE EDITOR: GERALDINE COLLINGE

BLACK
SPRING
PRESS

Published in 2003 by Black Spring Press Ltd
Burbage House
83–85 Curtain Road
London EC2A 3BS

in association with Apples & Snakes Ltd
BAC, Lavender Hill
London SW11 5TN
www.applesandsnakes.org

Apples & Snakes is funded by Arts Council England and Association of London
Government. The 21st birthday festival is supported with a grant from Arts Council
England. Apples & Snakes Ltd Charity Number: 294030

ISBN 0-948238-28-3

A full CIP record for this book is available from the British Library
A full CIP record for this book is available from the Library of Congress

Typeset in Palatino and Skia
Printed and bound by Cromwell Press Ltd, Trowbridge, England

Special thanks to:
Yvette Ankrah, Paul Beasley, Belinda Blanchard, Doug Bloom, Malika Booker,
Ruth Borthwick/Martin Calthorpe and the South Bank Centre, Darren Canady,
Christopher Cardale, Steve Carroll, Tasmin Chowdhury, Alison Combes and
Survivor's Poetry, Nicky Crabb, Cromwell Press, Bernie Cunnane, Joolz Denby,
Anna Goodman, Ghislaine Granger, Beth Grossman/Naomi Isaacs and the
Airlift Book Co, Robert Hastings, Erin Heinis, Jim and Sybil Hendrickson,
Jasper Jaymi Jinu, Linton Kwesi Johnson/Sharmilla Beezmohun, Suzy Joinson,
Hannah Jones, Gavin Joule, Louisa Kearney, Mimi Khalvati and the Poetry
School, KopyKat Printers, Segun Lee-French, Emile Sercombe, Jared Louche,
Jules Mann and the Poetry Society, Rupert Markland, Adrian Mealing,
Richard Michael, PR Murry, Mercy Nabirye, Monika Neall, Frederik Prausnitz,
Stuart Preston, Helen Riley and Manchester Poetry Festival, Rachel Rimmer,
Jacob Sam-La Rose and FYI, Sarah Sanders, Soho House London, Spread the
Word, Steve Tasane, Claude Ursarum, Dean Wakeling and Open Creatives,
Colin Watkeys, Mandy Williams... *and all Apples & Snakes staff, volunteers,
board members – past, present and future*

Contents

Foreword

Over the past two decades, Apples & Snakes has aimed to stretch the boundaries of poetry in performance and education, working across many art forms and commissioning artists to collaborate in new ways.

The evolution of Apples & Snakes has been both meteoric and methodical. In late 1982, a group of artists came together with the idea of breathing new life into London's performance poetry scene, with a particular focus on discovering new poets and increasing audiences for poetry. What began as a modest experiment in the Adam's Arms pub in Central London rapidly gained popularity – and occasionally notoriety – attracting superlative press and sell-out ticket sales. The company was soon supported by the GLC, which provided for artists fees, although initially the administration side continued to be carried by a dedicated but unpaid group of enthusiasts.

Apples & Snakes began to be invited to programme poetry events at arts centres, theatres and festivals across the UK, while always maintaining a series of regular events in London. In 1991 the company launched a Poets in Education Scheme, with help from Greater London Arts (later to become part of the Arts Council) and with it came the much-needed regular administrative funding. The education programme supported and subsidised artists undertaking work in schools, and a wide range of artists began to bring poetry into the lives of younger audiences. Today, every day of the year sees an Apples & Snakes' workshop in a London school, and many artists now earn a living from their poetry.

Apples & Snakes currently hosts a fortnightly series at London's Battersea Arts Centre, programmes poetry events all over the country and has coordinators in England's North West and East Midlands regions, aiming to have three more by 2005. Over the years, Apples & Snakes has mounted an astonishing array of tours, one-off events and artist commissions to produce new work.

As an organisation, Apples & Snakes has address the challenge to demystify poetry by staging events in unlikely places and with a range of unusual collaborators. For example, Bus Jam commissioned six poets to create a chorale work and perform it to unsuspecting passengers on South London buses, as well as a huge programme of work with community groups along those bus routes. Aisle 6 was a multi-disciplinary project combining the work of a textile designer, a photographer and a poet, which culminated in a performance in the Clapham Junction branch of Asda supermarket, alongside a group of local tea-dancers.

It was with a mixture of excitement and trepidation that we embarked upon the compilation of *Velocity* to celebrate our coming of age. We decided early on to limit submissions to artists who have performed for Apples & Snakes, and to include only work which was of the highest quality *off* the stage. This proved one of the most unexpected editorial difficulties – accepting that some of the very fine work we enjoy in performance derives too much of its power from the artist's theatrical skills to be comfortably confined to the page. On the other hand, some writers whom we had only known in a strong performance context surprised us with equally powerful, though quite different, work for the page.

Our next challenge came from another unexpected quarter: the layout of over a hundred artists' work in a single comprehensive volume. After much discussion, we decided that arranging the book alphabetically offered the least biased presentation, considering the huge variety of work. It felt imperative to limit our editorial influence to selecting the contents, while, from that point on, remaining as editorially invisible as possible. This had its drawbacks, for example when the majority of the visual contributions fell into the same two sections of the book, but on the whole, we felt that this route offered the reader the freedom to enjoy the anthology in small reads or cover to cover, or anything in between, without being led.

And finally a bonus legacy: in order to gather *Velocity* submissions from as wide a variety of sources as possible, we set ourselves the Sisyphean task of tracking down everyone who has ever performed for Apples & Snakes. This accidental adventure led us to some fantastic discoveries along the way, and has now sparked a whole new project: a web-based archive which is on-going, ever-evolving and open to suggestions and contributions from all of you.

Geraldine Collinge
Director, Apples & Snakes

Maja Prausnitz
Programme Coordinator, London

Chris Abani

Mary Magdalene as Marlene Dietrich

I
If God had any dress sense, he would look like this:
The blonde hair swept high and to the left.
The full red pout, the wrist teasing the world
With the Gitane smoldering like the slow fires of hell
And black. The suit. Or the bustier. And the hat.
And the voice calling like Ka from *The Jungle Book*:
"Trust in me, just in me, close your eyes, trust in me."

II
Haunting smoke-faded-velvet-curtained-cabaret-stages
Voice thick with the sediment of regret and squandered vice
Hooded lids, pursed lips and the cigarette, always the cigarette.
Could you bear to look into these eyes?
This body, once filled with the thick pulse of God's love
Veils a universe collapsed in on itself, like an endless night
Or the simple shadow cast on a tender shoulder by an earring.

Dannie Abse

Things

The strange, changing intimacy
of closely examined things
that studious painters know.
Dead caterpillars take wings.

Keepsake pebbles, exiled shells
looted from some holiday shore,
this mysterious giant key
that opens no familiar door.

So many things not wanted,
so many things outgrown:
a red uncomfortable chair,
an outdated telephone,
a vase in detestable taste
once won at an Easter fair.

A shiny suit, a discarded shoe,
clocks that no longer tick,
a broken musical box –
Frère Jacques, dormez-vous?

So many things finished and old
that make Time visible;
and nothing too useless
or graceless, or diminished
that cannot be tenderly painted
on a background of gold.

Shanta Acharya
Dear Customer

Be realistic and not too critical, bear in mind
that Boyfriend 5.0 was an entertainment package
but Husband 1.0 is an operating system.
A whole new concept; they cannot be compared.

Try to enter the command C: I THOUGHT YOU LOVED ME
when you switch Husband 1.0 on next, then install Tears 6.6.
Husband 1.0 should automatically run the following applications:
Guilt 7.0, Flowers 5.0, Dinner-At-Your-Favourite-Restaurant 3.0.
But remember, overuse of this application can cause Husband 1.0
to default to Grumpy Silence 2.0 or Happy Hour 4.0.

Note that Drinking Beer 6.0 is a disruptive programme,
generating Snoring Loudly files. DO NOT install
Mother-In-Law or another Boyfriend programme.
These are not supported applications and will crash Husband 1.0.
No amount of rebooting or repair can then restore the system.

It could also trigger Husband 1.0 to default to programme
Girlfriend 10.0 that runs dormant in the background.
It has been known to introduce potentially serious viruses
into the operating system. Husband 1.0 is a great programme,
but comes with limited memory; and has been known
to be rather slow in learning new applications.

You might consider buying additional software to enhance
system performance. Personally, I recommend Hot Food 4.0,
Single-Malt Scotch 5.0 supported by Black Satin Lingerie 6.0,
which have been credited with improved hardware performance.

Adisa

My Teddy Bear

My teddy bear has dreadlocks
Right down to the middle of his back
Each spiralling like a corkscrew
Tight springs painted black

Teeth gleaming like a carpet of snow
Marbles dipped in chocolate
Make my teddy bear's eyes
With his banana shape mouth
He always looks like he's just had a surprise

When he sleeps his mouth is always open
Like he's trying to catch flies

Walking slower than a tortoise
But with the bounce of a hare
Each stride he takes
He shouts,
"Somebody stop me if you dare!"

My teddy bear jives to jazz
Swings his hips to the soul
Spins on his head to hip-hop
Twists like an acrobat
When he hears rock and roll

Decked out in kente cloth
Like an Ashanti king
Robes of red, gold and green
Each finger is smothered in a gold ring   »

My teddy bear adores his food
Especially plantain and rice and peas
He does cartwheels backwards
For my mum's famous macaroni cheese
Polishing his plate squeaky clean
He lets rip a burp, louder than a clap of thunder
As he loudly proclaims, "Excuse me, please!"

My teddy bear is family
Much more than stuffing and fur
He's like my third brother
When I rub his head, I swear I hear him purr

We can not be separated
For together we are a team
The funny thing is, I can only see him
When I close my eyes to dream.

John Agard

Union Jack and Union Jill

Union Jack
and Union Jill
went up the hill
for a patriotic fling.

One waved a flag
and marched up and down.
One sang an anthem
and saluted after.

But they stole a quick kiss
as they talked politics
and soon love grew taller
than their raised fists.

For Union Jack
and Union Jill
the grass stood still
the hill hoisted its bliss

And they rolled over
in a peel of laughter
to find their convictions
lying in tatters.

Patience Agbabi

There Was an Old Woman Who Lived in a Shoe... ✢

1.
There was an old shoe, a lace-up, leather,
cracked by ambition, twisted by weather.
Black as a beetle dissected and bled.
Worn by the woman whose hair was dark red.

There was an old shoe that somebody buried
with a broken brown bottle for luck when they married.
Under the floorboards they laid down their roots.
The shoe gave birth to a pair of glass boots.

There was an old shoe, a laced-up space…
black leather walls draped with black leather lace,
black leather floorboards, a black leather shrine
where she knelt down to pray for a word, for a line.

There was an 'old' woman, 30 years-old
whose hair was the colour of antique gold.
She lived all her life in ambition's embrace.
You could almost decipher the lines on her face.

There was an old woman who lived in a Sh!
The twins are asleep. She was writing for two.
She prayed for red wine inspiration. She drank.
As her liver got bigger, the tiny room shrank.

There was an old bottle that met an old shoe.
She said, *I dare you* and he said, *I do.*
She said, *You're broken* and he said, *You're thin
as a rag.* She had bottle: he put the boot in.

»

A boot in her brain, and it grew and it grew
till the big black glass boot split into two.
Right brain, left brain, needle and thread,
they kicked and they danced themselves out of her head.

2.
There was an old woman who lived in her head
with black glass walls and a black glass bed
and a fibreglass lamp that went red, that went black,
that went red. On her scalp was a hairline crack,

a tiny thin line you could barely decode,
another, another, another. They flowed
like fine-lettered stitches, like intricate lace,
a row of black letters, a row of white space.

Her head got bigger, a balloon made of glass,
the black glassy walls became spider's web scars,
the floorboards groaned as if heavy with flood
till they smashed. And the red wine turned into blood.

They split her head open. They opened her head
like a book. Stitched her quiet with black leather thread.
She cried out in splinters, her tears bottle brown.
They took out the boots, stitched her up, held her down.

There was a glass box like an intricate mind
where the delicate pair of glass boots were enshrined.
She looks through the glass at each side of her soul.
She's writing but feels like she's shovelling coal.

There was an old woman: there was an old shoe.
She lived like a foot till the sole was worn through.
There was an old shoe and a narrative thread.
Her words are alive, and her story's undead.   »

3.
There was an old shoe with a stiff leather tongue.
There was an old woman, 30 years-young.
There was a brown bottle, empty and broken,
a pair of glass boots in a box they can't open.

There was an old woman who lived in a shoe.
Some of it, none of it, all of it's true.
She died alcoholic, she died in her bed,
She died when they severed the boots from her head.

* *There Was an Old Woman Who Lived in a Shoe was commissioned as part of the Faltered States performance project (2003), in which Apples & Snakes and the Science Museum asked five artists to visit the Museum's private collections and write about the objects they found there.*

Jamika Ajalon

On Nihilistic Adventure (notations)

I (in the beginning)
when I (we)
crash finally/
stars will spread
for an instant/
indelibly marking
some cerebral scream/
permanently on the face/of REALITY

II (real life TV)
collectively believed sensations
happiness = good episode on popular sit-cum-com/
REAL life is
perpetual purgatory
in-between shifts/in-between/jobs/weekends pre-ordained/pre-
fab/holidays/monday morning(s)/tragedies

III (material world)
possessions/a blinding-fold/barrier
to extreme (close-up) proximity to the street
rent unpaid/no friends family to speak of/a bed on the curb/
doorstep hovel sidewalk/any combination of these fine sub-
ground/sub-class accommodations

IV (lies stitched in time)
debtdebtdebt/recession
breaking/unemployment
decreasing/
a rise in joblessness/
stock markets disintegrate/
love on 14 feb/roses plunge (sink) in trade value/
as romance dies (kills)   »

V (stop the press)
evening standard
business section headlines/
war on drugs
drug testing
moral philandering/
political chap-stick/chapped-lipped politicians/
giving you a picture/media marketing/
freedom of speech/jerry springer's dick (cigar)/
the millennium bug up everybody's asses

VI (consume)
year 2002 what we gonna do
and 2003 what we gonna do
year 2004 what the hell we marchin' for/
genetically modified soil/
cell deterioration/
evolution/prices are rising/
helium balloon illusions
of progressed modernity/
post-modernity lies/expose themselves/
the superglue around the picture painted to be consumed

VII (still life)
pressure/erosion/slowly/subversive/still feeding/
hollow bone/injecting disease/muzaaak/transforming the
MASSES into numb pitted operational jelly babies/
minimal necesity for optimal brain soaks/
skinny dips in media
blitzes/just enough
pretty pictures on the office (cubical) walls/
and one slit on
the dark-painted doorway/
one slash of light
dripping red

Sara-Jane Arbury

The Pleasure Garden

Here
It takes ages
For ten minutes to
Meander by

Sitting square in the middle
Of a perfectly circular rug of grass
Thrown down by invisible hands

Fringed with nettles
And singed with a hole
Where a campfire smouldered
Long after the stories were over

So priceless
The temptation to spill myself
Overwhelms

It won't be long now...

Magic ruffles the edges
My hands grip on to air
Lungs billowing breeze
Heart racing to the finish
As this woven chaos soars
One degree further
Round the sun

I feel nothing but my body
Doing nothing but
Live

Steve Aylett
Brain a Goat Snappy

Jake used a hand-cranked rendering mill to produce a fab new magazine called *Brain a Goat Snappy*. The first edition was in fact a shallow pizza box containing a herd of killer bees. The headline on the cover shouted *INSIDE – KILLER BEES*, so when the creatures flew out and pelted the readers he could claim with closed eyes that they had been fully warned. The second issue bore the headline *INSIDE – KILLER BEES ON THE RAMPAGE*, and spoke mirthfully of the stress endured by the populace last time. The account was brought to life with vivid illustrations of O-mouthed fellows springing from armchairs in surprise at the approach of a bee – in order to make it clear that the object approaching was a bee, the illustrator had enlarged the insect to twelve times the size of the victim's head. Those scanning the account and its related diagrams were left in no doubt that an abomination had occurred, and Jake was arrested by a glass policeman full of sloshing liquid fat.

All copies of the first edition were clumsily confiscated and Jake's lawyer asked what he planned to say in his defence. "I will stand and glow," Jake said, "the wonder creeping abroad like a stench."

"But you smashed the cop and released the liquid fat," stated the lawyer, waving a tag of felt in Jake's face.

"Hello there," said Jake. In an effort to turn this remark to his advantage, Jake smiled at the lawyer in a way which suggested there was beauty in his arms, legs and motions.

"When you wrote that story about fluffy animals flying near people," said the lawyer, "did you think it was true?"

"I'm glad you noticed," said Jake, and realising this made no sense, hastily added "I love you" at a yell.

"I'm sorry Mr Fern," sighed the lawyer, closing his briefcase and shaking his head. "I now know what a monkey you are." He walked to the door and turned back momentarily. "Of course I'll bill you for the three hours we just spent chatting about energy fields." And he left, leaving Jake in his legal office.

Jake became instantly excited, frolicking amid the files and throwing stuff at the ceiling. But while scrabbling across a desk as though swimming, he managed to push himself out the window.

His next few issues of *Goat* contained the classic thoughtpiece *Twenty reasons why I don't push carrots into my eye* (being actually the statement "No time" repeated over and over) and the chicken series: *Interpreting chicken, Why nothing can prepare you for chicken, You are tailormade for chicken* and the final in the series, simply, *Horrorchicken*. His attempt to reach these heights again with *Why I will never be a Majorette, Welcome to my treachery* and *How to discern between me and your beautiful lover* were met with disappointment.

Desperate to boost circulation, Jake set up a problem page, and the first question he received was, "I have eaten a ton of lead. How many times have you done that?"

"Well, Seraphim," he replied, "many people see themselves as a dietary underclass because of this kind of practice, but not me. I can't get enough lead. In fact you'll likely find that your craving increases as the months and years pass. Crazy isn't it? My advice is to take a long hard look at yourself while spinning madly in a playground at night, while the rest of the world get on with their lives in a normal way. Looks like a crisis to me."

"I'm only really comfortable when screaming at cops," said another reader. "Is there something wrong with me?"

"You are loved," Jake replied.

Yet another reader stated, "I was cooking a lemon when it suddenly exploded and took away half my face. What do you think of that?"

"It depends how you look at it – is your face half there or is your face half gone?" He received a reply which re-stated that the man's face was half gone as a result of an explosion with a lemon. Abandoning the publication, Jake retreated to his diary: "Most people can't handle beauty. Bake me ten pounds. I know everything that's worth knowing."

He ran out with a spraycan, writing MY ARM IS AT AN ANGLE on a high wall. And he remained there for three days, trying to remember his name. Finally he went to a phonebox and called his mother, explaining he had to sign something. But of course he couldn't tell her who he was, beyond "Your fantastic boy."

"What's fantastic about you?" she asked.

"I'm learning to fend for myself."

"What else?"

"My legs are – wait, the money's running out!"

Calling back, he said, "My legs are long and tender, and I control them."

But he'd dialled a local building firm, and the reply he received was heart-breaking in its casual brutality. He wrote in his journal that evening:

I lost a licence in a field
I picked a weed and gave it in
The notion of successful stuff
Left me

Shamim Azad

Emptiness

Emptiness is:
When you wake up
    Early in the morning
        In your bed
            With your eyes shut
Your fingers, hands, arms, body, mind, and soul
Extend.
They grow and stretch
Like they never did.
They search and look for a touch desperately
But return without.

Francesca Beard

excerpt from *Chinese Whispers*

Light is an arrow, time is a shuttle
  – old chinese proverb

We're on Ladbroke Grove,
with the trees like saints in the dusty avenue,
and Jo asks me what I want.
I tell him, "Something bad for you… and American."
He disappears into Video Shack
with *Crouching Tiger, Hidden Dragon* twelve-quid overdue,
while I go on, through this melting part of the city.
Tower blocks tune jazz and geometry,
money suns itself in Georgian crescents.
The homeless guy who lives by Tesco
sprawls in a tall glass of gold
and salutes me, V for Victory,
as I pass through the sliding doors.

Inside, the air hums with choice.
If you are what you eat,
I'm a Rubik's Cube of biochemistry,
a consumer of international scandal,
a global cuckoo, diverting food
from other people's mouths to my sleek fridge.
Though I buy free-range eggs and fair-trade coffee,
it's too easy to feel guilty.
I feel a responsibility to our economy
to spend money on stuff.
And it's tough making decisions.
What do I want?
"Pick me, pick me," shine the fun-size lunchbox coxes   »

and the Danish bacon glistens fatly
and the South African Merlot winks ruby
and the French brie shrugs, "If you want."

I'm examining some vegetarian sushi
when a fight breaks out at checkout two.
"'Scuse me! Hello!" A man has queue-jumped.
Zig-zagged trolleys, jostling for position,
could just be an accident.
Still, it can't be allowed.
If he were sensible, he'd retreat
but he stands his stolen ground.
"Get back in your own line," shouts a matron in a sari.
The man retorts, "Get back to your own country."
Definitely the wrong thing to say.
The Filipina cashier squeaks in dismay.
The security guard with the tribal scars
pushes past Japanese art students.
The Australian chef from the Brazilian restaurant says,
"No offence, but you're out of line."
Three Jamaican women in three different queues
start shouting abuse in a Greek chorus of sisterhood.
The only English-looking guy, in an Italian suit,
organic chicken in his basket,
takes out his mobile and becomes invisible…
he's not really here at all – he's texting.
The queue-jumper senses it's not his crowd and leaves.
Everyone starts talking.

The chef asks me where I come from.
"Malaysia," I tell him.
"You're Muslim," he replies
and I say, "No, I'm Chinese Malaysian."
"Mee hao? Wau hern gkau shing?" he intones.
I freeze because I don't speak Chinese   »

but for some reason I can't just walk away
so my smile fixes into a grim rictus as his fades.
He's probably thinking that my expression
is politely inscrutable rage at this Foreign Devil
who's just called my ancestors
a herd of goat-fuckers by mistake,
when actually he's made a passable attempt at
"How's it going, mate?"
It's unfair, but I'm fed-up confessing that
I don't understand Cantonese or Mandarin –
people look at me like I've cut off my mother's tongue.
The chef slopes off with his basket of emergency lemons
and I'm marooned by the gift section.

There's an air plant, priced £2.99 –
an unprepossessing weed,
all wisps and drooping suspiration.
The tag says it gets its nutrients from air,
it's rooted nowhere.
But if it can't be planted, is it even a plant?
It's not in the flower section
with the heritage roses and the jade palace jasmine,
it's a Gift Section Misfit
shoved between the bath salts and the *I Love Mum* mugs.
Now I'm identifying with this weirdoid freak,
because if I was a plant, I'd be one of these,
sucking colour from anything I could.
In Britain today, it's all about roots, it's all about identity,
but there are banana bio yoghurts in aisle three
with more live culture than me.
I'm having a negative epiphany
in the dairy section of Tesco,
double disgrace to my race –
a crisis of Chineseness surrounded by cheese.   »

I dump my empty basket by the door
and exit fast onto Portobello Market,
straight into a walking Benetton ad.
People of all colours, creeds, nations,
stroll in the middle of the road, turning it pedestrian.
This is where I belong, in this privileged mix,
this moment of ordinary democracy,
this babelicious city,
where daily, more than 300 languages are spoken,
as diverse in their nature as the blue whale
to the fairy penguin, to the black panther
but each with something in common,
shared by no other animal communication system:
a grammar that allows one human to make
and another to understand a completely new observation,
an original thought, a statement
that no one else has ever said before.

I saw it on TV the other day...

*Chinese Whispers is a one-woman show written by Francesca Beard
from a collaboration with Arlette Kim George and Piers Faccini, which
was commissioned and developed by Apples & Snakes and BAC and
first performed at BAC, London in November 2003*

Beyonder

Let's Get Ready to Rumble (the radio edit)

Ladies and gentlemen,
welcome to Madison Satellite Garden on Moon Base Five
where we're coming to you live
for what can only be described
as the most anticipated fight this side of the Universe.

In the red corner we have the challenger,
weighing in at a combined weight
of approximately 780 billion pounds:
the horrifyingly humungous Humankind.

And in the blue corner we have the undisputed champion
of the first sector of the cosmos,
weighing in at an estimated weight of 650 trillion pounds:
the mercilessly masterful Mother Earth.

The referee, Time, calls both opponents together for a few words.
Humankind stares arrogantly at Mother Earth
oblivious of Time, clearly not hearing a word.
Both opponents now back up to their respective corners…

Ding!… Round 1

Humankind starts off this bout in fiercely aggressive fashion,
jabbing Mother Earth all over the body,
digging holes in pursuit of precious metals,
fossil fuels and all manner of valuable ores.
At this stage it looks like Humankind
is trying to dig down to Mother Earth's very core.

Looks like Mother Earth is slow to react,
her offensive mechanisms have yet to attack.
Humankind moves around with ease,
nimble and quick, he showboats,
promising this bout will be a breeze.   »

Wait, what's this? Humankind seems to have set his own rules.
He's got Mother Earth by the throat, choking her full of fumes,
burning fossil fuels at a rate of knots,
gassing her repeatedly with the release of CFCs.

Ding!...

At this point, ladies and gentleman,
let's hear a word from our sponsors,
CQ Intergalactic Petroleum:

We'd like to thank our viewers for participating
in the breaking down of so many Ecosystems
and the building up of our bank balance
and look forward to your continued custom...

Ding!... Round 2

Now, Mother Earth is showing her aggressive side,
peeling back her ozone layer
to expose Humankind to the wrath of her ally, Sunshine.

Humankind cowers back for a moment,
then blindly continues his attack,
sucking up the excess radiation
with no thoughts of the mutated future.

But Mother Earth is picking up her game,
calling forth the powers of the universe as she begins to take aim,
releasing armies of tsunamis, she lambastes Humankind,
wave upon wave crashes down.

Mother Earth now takes centre stage,
melting her ice caps, bringing forth floods and disease.
The raining blows force Humankind down to his knees,
not begging for a reprieve, just looking to land a low blow,
aiming shots at Mother Earth's waterworks
as he pollutes her rivers and seas.

Ding!...

Don't go away folks, we'll be right back
after this short commercial break from
Dumping Grounds Anonymous 'R' Us: »

We pay cash and you take our toxic trash!
Please note, we are not liable
for any future deformities experienced
Contact us on freephone 0800 666…

Ding!… Round 3

And Mother Earth is out in a flash – flood,
hurricanes and typhoons bring down mudslides.
Humankind gets buried beneath an avalanche of blows.
Will he be able to overcome this onslaught
as he bounces off the ropes?

Humankind turns away in pain and
Mother Earth pounds him with another blow.
What a combination there, ladies and gentleman,
a western earthquake followed by an eastern monsoon!

Humankind flies through the air but luckily lands on his feet
Slow and now wilting, Humankind attempts a retreat…
This is incredible! He's running from Mother Earth!
Unbelievable – he's exiting via space station 2-0-1-2.

There's pure pandemonium here at
Madison Satellite Garden,
But let's speak to the champion Mother Earth.

Well, Mother Earth,
your granite chin pulled you through –
how did you find the fight?

"Thanks, Time!
I knew I had him from the beginning
because when I hit him he screamed like a little girl.
Every time I unleashed a bit of power
all I heard was 'life's so brutal!' and 'why me?'
So it was only a matter of biding my time…"

Ladies and gentlemen, I give to you the winner
and still undisputed champion
of the first sector of the cosmos:
Mother Earth!

Paul Birtill
Fella Meets Girl, Falls in Love

Laughing bathing exercising
Clean underwear...

Checks his bank balance
Tries for promotion
Buys a jacket
Washes his car...

Shows off, tells lies
Distrusts his mates
Thinks about his dead mother
Kids, log fires, growing old together...

Stops getting drunk
Goes to church
More exercises
More baths
Fresh jokes and confectionary...

Takes her to family home
Shows her his old bedroom
Old toys first school book
Park where he played
Hundreds of snaps and
Mother's grave...

Strolls around the neighbourhood
Holding her hand for all to see
What a find, an acquisition
Mine all mine, aren't I clever...   »

Discovers she's a lesbian
Never thought to ask
Reverts to a four year-old
Stamps his feet yells
Hits her, digs up his mother's
Grave and sends her the bones...

Paul Birtill

Counting for My Life

Sitting in my local pub
I find myself counting the number
Of candles on tables and imagine
They are the years I have left to live.
But seven is not enough – so I stare
Down at the floor and count the number
Of discarded fag-ends – though nine
Is still too short – so I turn my
Attention to the spirit bottles
Behind the bar and with some relief
Count fourteen – that's more like it.

Valerie Bloom

A Thousand Years

And he laid hold on the dragon, that old serpent, which is the Devil,
and Satan, and bound him a thousand years. [Rev. 20:2]

Across the vast expanse of earth,
Backwards and forwards he went,
And he called and halloed, "Is there anyone there?"
Till his voice and his courage were spent,
As he shook the lifeless bodies,
Turned each one in despair,
His echo came back to haunt him,
"Is there anybody there?"
And he raised his head in the silence,
Up to the empty sky,
Hoping to see a bird, or a plane,
Or an insect flying by.
But the air was void of life form,
Not even a vulture wheeled
Over the rotting carcasses.
His searching eyes revealed
Only the black face of heaven,
Frowning at his call,
He gazed at the chaos around him
Knew there was no further to fall,
Mountains which once towered skywards
Had been torn out of the ground,
Villages, towns and cities,
Hills and rocks were strewn around,
There was nothing left, not a trickle
Of the rivers and the seas,   »

And the matchsticks lying beneath his feet,
Were all that was left of the trees.
He turned, walking on a roadway of bodies,
His distress too deep for tears,
Knowing he'd live to regret what he had done,
For a thousand lonely years.

Valerie Bloom

I Travelled to a Far Country

I travelled to a far country,
In a boat made out of wood,
A multitude travelled beside me,
The evil and the good.

The healthy and the infirm
Sailed with me in matching boats,
Silence and darkness were the seas
Which kept our crafts afloat.

We found when we got in the boats,
We'd lost the gift of speech,
And so we could not say goodbye,
To those left on the beach.

We found when we got in the boats,
That we could see no more,
And so we knew not of the tears
Shed by those on the shore.

We found when we got in the boats,
That none of us could hear,
So we were oblivious of the wails
Of those along the pier.

We sailed for many moonless nights,
And so we gained the patience,
To serve that country's black-robed king,
And obey his laws of silence.

Valerie Bloom

Strange

There are two giant lobsters
Talking on the telephone,
An Alsatian is evolving
Out of a marrowbone.

A man stands by the window
In his birthday suit,
A preacher is being split in two
By a twisting oak tree root.

A woman tears her insides out
And drops them in a pail,
A giant snake devours himself
Beginning at his tail.

A light bulb flickers on and off
Inside an empty room,
A girl sits counting marbles
In a superman costume.

In a basin on a table,
Is a liver and a heart,
And the people, dumb with wonder,
Stand and stare at Modern Art.

Jean 'Binta' Breeze

excerpt from Apples & Snakes' *Dancing on White Sand*, 23.5.03 *

I started writing poetry when I was about eleven years-old in high school in Jamaica. Before that from the age of five, I grew up in a little village in the mountains of Western Jamaica called Patty Hill, which wasn't far away from Flower Hill, and every concert that we had for the church or for the school was what we called a penny concert. Cause there was no funding agencies, there was no arts councils so in order to fund our basic school or primary school or church, we had concerts and we had to pay a penny to put someone up to sing a song, if you knew they could sing or if you they couldn't sing and then you'd pay like two pennies to take them down. So whatever you were good at, from very early, was what you did.

And when I was a little girl, I had an incredible mother. She knew all these poems off by heart and from when I was about five and able to get on the stage and recite poems, that's what I did to make money for the primary school, for the church. Now one of the first poems that my mother taught me was:

An old man going alone high way
Came at the evening cold and grey
To a chasm vast and deep and wide
Through which was flowing a swollen tide
The old man passed to the other side
That swollen stream had no fear for him
But he turned when safe on the other side
And built a bridge to span the tide
Good friend, said a fellow pilgrim near,
Why waste ye your strength in building here
Your journey will end with the ending day

You'll never again pass this way
You've crossed the chasm vast and wide
Why build ye here at even tide
The builder lifted his old grey head
Good friend, in the past I've come, he said
There comes after me today a youth whose feet
Must pass this way
He too must cross in the twilight dim
Good friend, I'm building this bridge for him

And that was one of the first poems I ever learned, and I've been reciting it since I was five. I was lucky enough to grow up in a culture where poetry was spoken and not on the page. I didn't have books of these poems; my mother taught them to me. When I was ten, there was a rally amongst all the Baptist churches in Western Jamaica and I was chosen to learn Rudyard Kipling's *If*.

These were the poems I grew up on, because of church, because of school – this was Jamaica. And so at the same time, every Jamaican child knew a Louise Bennett poem. She was the only poet working in the Jamaican language and bringing it to the stage. So she did poems, for example, about domestic workers, because lots of women in Jamaica work as domestic workers.

And that was what it meant to be Caribbean. It was learning Kipling beside Louise Bennett. Growing up in a rural village, born of peasant grandparents and understanding what the joy was of being a community: giving voice, nothing elitist, nothing not understood, nothing obscure, a real sense of rhythm and rhyme.

And so I left from all of that and went into high school after I passed what was the eleven-plus. There I met TS Eliot... And we dubbed TS Eliot! We rapped TS Eliot and that was the brilliance of being a Caribbean person!

When I was about eleven, I started writing for the high school magazine and writing poems like *Post Mortem*: "And after death what shall we do?..." My English teacher, who was on contract, having just graduated in English from Oxford University and wanting a few years abroad, said to me, "Oh, you must have read Dante's *Inferno*." Never heard of it, but that was where we were in Jamaica at that time.

I was born in 1956; Jamaica got independence in 1962. At the same time, there was cricket, so you know, we were *beating England at cricket* – eventually. And getting our own back. It was like a very nice way of working out Empire. But what Empire did not understand was the fact that this great migration of West Indian people were going to arrive in Britain – and that in 2003, the Battersea Arts Centre would look like *this*. That is the result of Empire.

For those few years after independence, when we realised that we had been handed over the government but not the economics, in the same way that Mandela was handed over the South African government but the finance minister had to be of their national party and white. So you learned from the start that they will give you anything – the dress, the ceremony, the pomp – but never the money, never the bank account. We started thinking, it's time to make certain changes in Jamaica. We have been independent since 1962 and there are things we can do.

At the beginning of the '70s , we used to have those 45 records, that had one song on the A-side and another song on the B-side. Well, in Jamaica they said, "No more song on the B-side. Let's give an instrumental version of the A-side on the B-side." DJs would play the A-side and then flip it over to the B-side, take the microphone and start ad-libbing about whatever they wanted to say. And poets in the early '70s, both in London, like Linton Kwesi Johnson, and in Jamaica, like Mutabaruka and me, we all started chanting – and so dub poetry was born.

Dub poetry was serious, because we weren't publishing books or reading in libraries. We were making records and performing in a band before ten-thousand people, so you couldn't get up there with a book to read from and talk about how bad you felt about your father beating you when you were a child. There was poetry of the public voice, poetry of the political movement and poetry that took part in the community or what the community was suffering or undergoing.

When I started reading in 1976, it was after the first government of Michael Manley and the PNP had declared themselves Socialists, and for the first time there were policies. For example, most domestic workers were women and they were awfully paid and treated really badly. For the first time, a law came with minimum wage that applied to female domestic workers. Before that, we didn't get married, we had children out of wedlock, so we were bastards. It was the first time a government came in and said, "There are no bastards. Even if you are not born in wedlock, you have the right to inherit." These were the changes that were happening – hospitals, schools being built.

Coming out of the '60s into the early '70s, Nina Simone singing *Young, Gifted and Black,* Angela Davis coming out and saying, "Yes, we're going to make Jamaica a revolutionary place," Bob Marley began to sing for the people; all the energy of the people began to focus.

In those days I used to be the poet who came on at political rallies after the guest speaker had given his speech. At that time we were taking over the plantation lands from all those who had gone abroad, and giving them over to peasants to grow their yams or their peas and things like that. So I was writing poems about things like that.

But at that time, the voice in dub poetry, the voice in a lot of politics, was male. So when I came onto the scene, the first thing they said was, "You're playing them songs like a man because a woman only writes love poetry." That was the first criticism. Mutabaruka was the first one who said, "OK, I'll call you because you're talking politics." Come 1978, America didn't like the fact that we became Socialists and opened contacts with Cuba and so on, so the foreign press gave us such a bad write-up that all the tourists stopped coming to Jamaica, all the business people started moving their money out of Jamaica, into America. The economy collapsed, and by 1978 we had to sign with the International Monetary Fund. So, it's been 400 years from the plantation whip to the International Monetary Fund grip.

Aid travels with a bomb, watch out, aid travels with a bomb.
And for countries in despair, aid for countries that have no share
They are dumping surplus food in the sea,

Yet they can't allow starvation to be and
Aid travels with a bomb, watch out, aid travels with a bomb.
They buy your land to dump nuclear waste
You sell it so that food your children can taste and
Aid travels with a bomb, watch out, aid travels with a bomb.
You don't know if they are on CIA fee or even with the KGB
Cause you think your country is oh so free
Until you look at the economy and
Aid hits you like a bomb, watch out!

That was 1978 – but look at Iraq now. Look at all the problems in Iraq. Look at all the multi-national companies getting billion-pound contracts in Iraq, all of them American. That poem is as relevant today as it was in 1978.

By 1981 I'm chanting these lyrics and Linton Kwesi Johnson arrives to do a concert with us in Kingston for the BBC. He invited some of us back to London – Oku Onuora, Mutabaruka and, in 1985, he invited me.

I arrived on Railton Road in Brixton and saw a sign saying *Cultural Centre,* so I thought, drums and folk music. I walked in there – pure gangsta gambling! When I went back to Linton, he said, "You're lucky you weren't mugged." I said, "Oh, so that's a cultural centre in Brixton!" My first five years were amazing! There was an international book fair of Third World Latin writers. There was Ntozake Shange. There was the ANC from South Africa. There was a Muslim movement. Everyone gathered in London for that. It was an incredible time to arrive.

But all that collapsed at the end of the '80s – remember, by the end of the '80s, there had been ten or more years of Thatcher, Reagan and Seaga in Jamaica. So things were like dead and that kind of Black political movement fell apart. What I found left was that Black women, all women, but more certainly black women, started buying books, started coming to poetry readings, started gathering about the politics of their situation. And that's why someone like me survived where a lot of male poets did not survive.

In 1985 Apples & Snakes were just at their beginning, looking for funding, trying to keep performance poetry alive, bringing poets as soon as we arrived. They said, "Come and do a gig for us." That's seventeen years ago and look at the work that Apples & Snakes has done all through that time, all over this country, introducing new voices all the time, bringing them together with old voices so that the history is not lost. That is what I'm now a part of, being here tonight in 2003. And it's even more personal than that.

When I came in 1985, Paul Beasley was in charge of Apples & Snakes and, because people here knew me performing on that platform, they called up Apples & Snakes to see if they could book me. When he left that job and someone else took over, I said to Paul, "Keep on doing what you're doing, baby!" Fifteen years on, Paul is still my agent and a really good friend.

This is what I mean about history, because I go into schools now and the students don't know who Linton Kwesi Johnson is. They don't listen to him. Where is that link of the last fifteen years that says we're not lost? Why has the British voice, especially the Black-British voice, become American rather than Black-British? Why aren't we speaking in our own accents, with our own rhythms, with our own sounds of where we come from and what it means to be here and to dare to say it's different from anywhere else?

But seriously I think that Apples & Snakes is one of the few – if not the only – institutions that has stood the test of that seventeen years as I have seen it. Apples & Snakes continues to bring new voices with old voices, giving a sense of the history of where they are coming from. To be here, any time they call me to come and perform here, is a pleasure and an honour because I know the kind of audience who will be here.

this is a transcription of Jean 'Binta' Breeze's performance at Apples & Snakes' Dancing on White Sand show, 23 May 2003 at BAC, London. Only illustrative poems have been omitted.

Pete Brown

House by the Airport

Got a house by the airport
I watch the planes
They ebb and flow
When they come back to land
They fly so slow
Big tired birds
Still wired from their trip through time
Those angry eyes that stare through mist and snow
There are no words…

Got a house by the airport
And there's a girl
Looks after me
When troubles come my way
She soothes my mind
Long caring hands
Sharing me alongside all my ghosts
The wild songs they play still sound so fine
Hey listen man…

Got a house by the airport
In case the moment's
Ever ripe
When someone calls me up
And says, "Come on,
We need you now
Old crazy head
Get blowing with your loaded axe
Scare up some echoes, bring the sunburst down
And raise the dead…"

Dana Bryant

Loulou on the Train

There is the Hudson river in the middle of the day
there is the beauty of the sun on the water
the trees
the houses whizzing by
the light on the river
the beauty of the river
the mountains in the distance

surely there is nothing more beautiful than this
train
far away from all which seemed real yesterday
real
and you are racing away
to that which is good
today
you will make it happen there
you will bring it to bear there
you will take advantages
gain
you will make loving friends
There's something

you're writing about the river
and the boats in the harbor
and Loulou a litle girl of two
talks to her father in the seat
in front of you
making up stories about
inside of here   »

there is something special
beautiful
she loves her daddy
she loves the city
she loves the trees
the stillness
he loves her
he lives inside the
truth of Loulou
he is in love
with the woman
who is his wife
who has given him
a daughter
someone
a constant surprise
who he really deeply loves
there is a strong similarity
his soft hands
hers
make her real
little munchkin
she is sweet
she is someone
who looks at the sun
directly
she speaks
all the time
she's a little munchkin
how can he listen to it
all the time
her high pitched squeak
unless he makes it his business
to make her real
for himself

»

there is something to
having a someone
make sure
there's a place for you
a seat
on the train

you're looking at the lake
the churches
the river
the trees
the beautiful Hudson River Valley
here for centuries.
Croton Harmon
he took you there
he was best in the evenings
when you were tired
fed up with your day
but the kind of man who couldn't
go farther
in the way you
keep digging around
to bring the humanity of
that lost something
inside yourself
there's something
recognizable
nothing wrong
with
must be found
little ghost girl
nothing wrong
with trying to find
a lost piece of

»

you can write and
think
at the same time
there's no love
for you out there
you feel like
there's no love
somehow you feel
as if there is something
out there
keeping you from being
with yourself

it's not about the privileges
of various and sundries
so much as the fact
that there must
be
in the world
someone
who understands you
completely
tolerates you absolutely
lets you grow
is determined to embrace
you
bring things back into perspective
lets you breathe
breathes without
taking the breath out of you
lets you live
takes care
to take good care
of you
takes you to a movie   »

in Midtown Manhattan
in the middle of rush hour
and finds a parking space
pays attention
gets on with it
does away with
there's...
something
able to explain the sun
the Hudson River
the changing of the seasons
the gift of new friends
forever
fiercely
never letting you go
putting you to bed
loves you more than Love itself
loves you
makes changes in the world
on your behalf
making room for you
somehow
mysterious
who thinks the world of you
who thinks the world of you
just because you're there

Ainsley Burrows

Let's Pretend

Let's pretend
we didn't leave codes and rivers
collard greens and gumbo
grits and a parallel universe
Vietnam hallucinations of Garvey
wrapped in barbed wire
Like y'all ain't never heard bones speak
blood and sweat curdled on leg-irons
throat shackles
bleed me a history book
of granulated sugar and cotton gins
smoke huts and crushed spines
molested minds and charity rapes of
African souls on European pallets
MIT and Harvard
can explain nuclear fission
but they can't explain the Harlem Shake
Atlantic fever
Goree Island gone mad
broke his neck twelve times in twelve places
he's the Zodiac sign on ridlin
a galaxy with a speech impediment
handcuffed to a nightstick
and
most of our magicians
were murdered
during the middle passage
because
most of our magicians

»

took their drums on board
a small caption
"time-control history reversal museum"
For sale
two Negroes and a drum
that bends space
reorganizes reality
Watch time mutate
rock and roll slave ship
funky dungeon
Beat box, break beats,
back beats, broken backs
Sweating tobacco stains
skating until our cells divide
Blue
swing until our mothers remember
Swing like 100 years of lynching
Swing until our children remember
that hip-hop was invented by white men
in slave quarters
Remember the unreported uprising
Remember that there are star systems
in your spirit
That it is possible to dream even
when you are dead
That there are remnants of futures
in the conscience of your blood
tapping visions into wood
We suffered in silence
Swing
backs to audiences
guitars on fire
fist in the air
We howled and screamed   »

until our gums bled
Burning crosses
and vacant lunch counters
We'll feed her back to them encrypted
like someone crashed a slave ship
into the Pentagon
And disaster comes
blind like 19,000 light years
dressed in red
making promises to Wall Street
Found a stock quote in a rain drop
They'll send helicopters and war planes
But how will they stop us
When we are 90% liquid
And 99% space

Billy Childish

Billy Childish

where eccentrics fear to tread

in this town
where
the grey faces of 15 year-old whores
light the night streets

and
drunken mothers
with babes in arms
spit on the backs of hunch-backed women
on night buses
who are then in turn
beaten around the head with bottles

and
in multi-storey car parks
where rubber johnnys are spilled to the ground
and squaddies have their ears bitten off
and spitten to the ground
and lovers leap
and
the sky smashes into the hillsides

and
all the while
there is still miraculous
silence
and peace
and space and joy

where
van gogh once stepped
and
eccentrics fear to tread

Billy Childish

Billy Childish

we have war because we love war

because we
want to push
to the front
and
have
all the prizes
to ourselves

because love
is not enough
nor
are
new cars
or out of town shopping complexes
or mobile phones
or surround-sound stereos
or 60-inch television screens
or ready-prepared meals
or holidays in other peoples misery
or jesus
or buddha
or being able to eat smoke and drink ourselves to death
then cry that our hospitals are all shit

because
we
need
to feel slighted
and
peeved
by the least inconvenience
of the day

»

because the sun is not right
or our shoelaces are too tight
or
because
we hate our mothers
or our fathers
or our wives
or our sisters
or our brothers
or teachers for failing us
or people for failing us
or just life
or husbands
or the sky
or the rain
or our bosses
or our children
or our work mates
or paedophiles
or the mad
or car drivers
or pedestrians
or people on bikes
or people wearing the wrong type of hats
or the wrong shoes
or smoking cigarettes
or not smoking cigarettes
or drinking
or not drinking
or foreigners
or fascists
or policemen
or peace marchers
but
ultimately
ourselves

Billy Childish

Lana Citron

Agnes and the Camel-Coloured Coat

One late and desolate winter afternoon, Agnes Partridge, swathed in her newly acquired coat, gingerly stepped off the number 19 bus. She paused a moment to admire her reflection in the glass of the bus shelter and postured as would a fashion model, with lips pouting, cheeks sucked in and her right arm bent at the elbow.

"My, my, but don't I only look the business," she thought to herself, and as if reading her mind, the bus conductor declared, "Agnes, you're a sight to behold."

Blushing, she gushed, "Go away with you, Maurice."

"Sure, if I weren't a respectable married man, I'd be down on my knees proposing," he flirtingly ventured, and Agnes, aghast at such a suggestion, cried,

"Maurice Flathery!" adding coyly, "And if I weren't a respectable married woman, I'd be down there with you."

Maurice pulled the chord signalling the driver to move on, then blew Agnes a wild kiss. Smiling coquettishly, she watched the bus trundle off into the distance, before twirling around so that the skirt of the pure wool, camel-coloured coat did lift and tease her stockinged knees. Its weave was so fine, it could easily have been mistaken for cashmere, so soft on the tips of her fingers, and Agnes ran her hands lightly down over her huge breasts and stout round belly, in awe of her own fancified beauty.

Agnes had first spied the coat in the cafe of Exclusivity, the most exclusive department store in town. She had been sipping tea and nibbling a Danish pastry with her best friend and neighbour, Myrtle, when she glanced it from a distance. It was pushed to the forefront of a designer rail and hung resplendent in its polythene casing, but barely visible, due to Myrtle's hairstyle, which had been set to resemble a helmet shape.

"I had a lovely bit of meat off of Bert the other day," Myrtle remarked to her friend.

"Hm, yes, yes," Agnes muttered, shifting in her seat to better fix her view.

"A delicious piece of beef. You're a lucky woman being married to a butcher."

"Well, Myrtle, I daresay that's true."

"A tender rump... Agnes? Agnes, are you listening?"

Agnes peered distractedly over Myrtle's shoulder, then jumped up and out of her seat.

"Myrtle, I've just seen the most glorious coat," she proclaimed, and quite forgetting the remaining half of her pastry, Agnes zig-zagged her way through the cafe and sped over to the fashion floor.

"Oh, for God sake," grumbled Myrtle.

Agnes had always been unable to contain her impulses and, unfastening her handbag, Myrtle wrapped the remaining piece of pastry in a paper napkin and popped it in her bag. Meanwhile, Agnes had reached the rail where the coat hung, and eager to try it on she hailed the attention of a young sales assistant. The assistant, busy chatting on the phone, ignored her. "Dear Lord," Agnes sighed, wondering how such an inexperienced salesgirl could be put in charge of such fine merchandise. A coat as exquisite as the one before her could easily be lifted off the rails, or mistakenly ruined by clumsy handling, especially the sticky hands of a Danish pastry nibbler. The thought lay uncomfortably in her mind, and she double-checked her own fingers before taking the coat off the rail. Turning sharply, her chin pointing upward, Agnes stormed by the assistant into the changing room, with Myrtle following close on her heels.

Her own coat, an old checked tweed item that had seen better days, was hastily discarded onto the floor. Agnes clucked with glee, lifting off the polythene cover to touch, for the first time, the texture of the coat's material beneath. Gently, she let her fingers trace over the still-pockets, and then eased each button open, slipping her hand inside, to feel the silky smoothness of the lining. Her right arm delved into one sleeve, her left into the other, and she shivered with joy, noticing the weight of the coat bearing down upon her. Then, fastening it about her, her fingers delicately pushed the buttons back through each button hole, till finally, like a young girl in the first flush of love, she turned to face herself in the mirror.

How perfectly it fit and she lifted up her arms, to make sure the material didn't pull across her generous chest. Even the length suited, delighting her ankles by flirting with her shins.

"I'll definitely take it. It's me. I feel a million dollars," gasped Agnes. "I'll definitely take it." The sales assistant, having finished her phone conversation, pulled back the curtains of the dressing room and stood complimenting Madame on her discerning taste.

"Well, yes, it's true, I do have an eye for things."

"Oh, Agnes, do be sensible." Myrtle quipped, "It most probably costs an arm and a leg."

She grabbed the sales ticket to examine it closely and then declared triumphantly, "Aha, what did I tell you? A small fortune."

The most beautiful coat of the season was priced accordingly.

"But Madame, it looks as if it were tailored to fit," lauded the assistant. "And it is an exclusive. Well, almost, for there is only one other of its like in the whole of the country."

Myrtle remained unimpressed. Such a ridiculous amount of money to be spent on a coat and she made her feelings known. "Agnes, I'm sure there are other coats, much cheaper and perhaps not so flattering, but just as good. Good enough for you."

And to further prove her point, she begged Agnes to reconsider.

"Camel is a very hard colour to wear and I'm not entirely convinced it suits your wan and lacklustre complexion."

Agnes would not be put off.

"Myrtle, I am going to get this coat and that is that," Agnes declared, startled by her own sense of conviction. Slowly, she peeled the coat off her shoulders and, handing it to the assistant, assured her, she would return to collect the coat in four weeks.

Sure enough, four weeks later, after much scrimping and saving, Agnes boarded the bus into town, clutching her handbag close to her side, ready to collect the coat.

With precision, Agnes counted out the money in front of the assistant and decided she would wear it home. Ah, how high her spirits did soar and, tootling on her way, she noticed many heads turn her direction, for indeed the camel-coloured coat stood out against the grey backdrop of the city. How proud her husband, Bert, would be. No doubt he would think he was one of the luckiest men alive. Agnes had not mentioned the coat to Bert, although the night before, whilst polishing Bert's boots, she had let slip she had a surprise in store for him. Bert loved surprises, and Agnes loved surprising him.

Turning from the bus shelter, Agnes passed the corner shop, catching the eye of Jack Daley, the owner, who was sweeping the porch.

"That's a grand coat you're wearing, Agnes," he hollered out to her.

"Thanks, Jack. It's new."

"Woman, you look bewitching. Sure, I've half a mind to get inside it with you."

"Wash out your mouth with soap and water... You oul' teaser," giggled Agnes, delighted with all the attention being lavished on her. She couldn't wait to show it off to Myrtle, and she skipped round the corner and on down the road. Myrtle was certain to steam with vexation at the sight of it. Indeed, if the truth be known, Myrtle had a nasty streak of jealously running through her, and would inevitably want whatever Agnes had, the same, if not better.

As she passed by the community centre, a notice pinned to the door stalled her. *Auditions for the Xmas Panto. Little Red Riding Hood. To be held next Thurs. All welcome.* For fifteen years, Agnes had been an active member of the local dramatics society, appearing in all the productions, and had played the lead on several occasions. Casting herself in the role of Miss Hood, Agnes let loose the reigns of her imagination. There she was, in her camel coat, wandering through the forest on her way to Granny's, her handbag swinging at her side. And there was Myrtle, not to be outdone, playing the wolf. Ha! And as for Bert? Agnes saw her husband dressed in his butcher's apron, with his shotgun thrown over his shoulder, riding high on a trusty steed, a rose stuck between his teeth and on his way to rescue her. Transfixed by such reveries, she outwardly sighed, "Bert... Bert..."

"Agnes... Agnes?" The intrusive voice of Father Phillips interrupted her kindling fantasy. "Agnes, I take it you'll be auditioning this year?"

"Oh, Father, I... I wouldn't miss it for the world."

"And would I be right in thinking you're wearing a new coat?" asked the priest, flaring his nostrils in approval.

"Yes, Father."

"Very nice it is, so it is."

"Why, thank you, Father," Agnes replied in a half whisper.

Unable to resist the temptation, Father Phillips gently laid his hand on her left shoulder. "Very becoming. Like a vision."

"Well, best be off, Father. I've to call in on Myrtle."

Father Phillips removed his hand. "Right you are. See you next week, so."

Agnes walked the short distance to Myrtle's front door and knocked gently. She waited patiently, swaying from side to side, enjoying the flow of the material brushing against her thighs and the warmth of the coat upon her shoulders. There came no reply, so she opened the door, it being the good old days when doors were points of welcome. Then, about to holler out Myrtle's name, she came upon a sight so shocking that she froze in total disbelief, before spinning on her heels to run next door and fetch her husband's shotgun.

Bert's gun was kept for safety's sake, behind the top of the wardrobe, in the master bedroom. Up on her tippy toes, Agnes reached as far as she could, stretching up her chubby little arms, and took down the large black shotgun. Of all her husband's possessions, this surely bought him the greatest of joys. Every other weekend, Bert, soiled and smelling of earth, would return after a good day's hunt, whereupon Agnes would bustle him into the small back kitchen, with its large pots of boiling water, ready for his bath. She would help undress him, his clothes thick with mud, and then, when he was quite naked and submerged in the hot, steamy suds, he would point to his gun and request Agnes polish it for him. Immediately Agnes would whip out her chamois cloth and diligently begin.

With the gun now in her hands, Agnes thought only of the wicked sight she had witnessed in Myrtle's hallway. Slipping the leather strap over her shoulder, she hastily descended the stairs and ran next door. Quietly, she pushed open the front door and, peering anxiously inside, her suspicions were once again confirmed. In Myrtle's hallway, at the foot of the stairs, lay a pair of bloodied boots, familiar boots, leaning against an Exclusivity bag.

A lump then rose in Agnes's throat, on hearing what sounded like the stifled squeals of Myrtle coming from the bedroom above. A shudder, the like of which Agnes had never experienced, ran through her spine. Clutching the gun ever more closely, she eased back the safety latch, her finger curled around the trigger, and crept up the stairs, silent as a spectre. Slowly, she inched toward the bedroom, petrified of confronting the truth. The shotgun lay prone in her arms, and she cocked the muzzle in readiness. Then, throwing open the door, Agnes swallowed hard at the sight affronting her gaze, and her finger pulled on the trigger, not once, but twice.

Two shots rang out on that cold and desolate afternoon, the first shot striking to the heart of Bert; as for the second, it was destined to travel through Myrtle's mouth, which gaped open in terror. However, just before the shot exploded Myrtle's brains out over the padded headboard, Agnes cried out, "This time, Myrtle, you've gone too far."

For there, hanging resplendent in front of Myrtle's wardrobe, was the second camel coat.

So it happened, Agnes, wearing her new camel-coloured coat, killed the two people closest to her. Luckily the coat did not bear a trace of murder upon it. Agnes lay the gun across the bed, having given it one last polish, and then, without much ado, she left.

The light outside had diminished, and already she could see the first glimmer of heavenly stars.

John Cooper Clarke
Eat Lead, Clown

It was time to move. I pulled on a raincoat, put away a pep pill, set fire to a cigarette and split.

Outside the stars stuck out of the sky like dandruff specks on a purple tux and the moon spat blue light on the nightlife.

I stopped at a vacant hub-cap to check out my wardrobe, the 2-tone dexters in particular. Someone strangled a saxophone… elaborately.

Enter the brothers Archangelo, two Brilliantine gypsies, rats on rollerskates, the plague on wheels.

Frankie fingered a string of powder-blue rosary beads while Angelo carried a switch.

I swerved, missed out on a set of signet rings and came back with a jap chop to the breadbox. Angelo slashed my wrist before catching a dexter in his wheels. The show was over, and I called the shots.

Blots of blood the size of pennies hit the pavement, peppered with rosary beads, forming an epileptic colour scheme. The flames of doom shot forth from a tightened grip. I gazed on the filth of the world and my heart said nothing.

The sound of squealing brakes and the smell of rubber vied for attention. A sideways focus revealed a sky-blue Bel Aire deluxe convertible rocking on the springs.

"Get in, Jim," said a voice from a thousand fathoms.

Her lips were a poisonous pink; she looked like St Theresa of the Roses in one of her cheesier moments.

I was bleeding all over the fake leopard upholstery.

We stopped outside the Chevron Burgerama, its synchronised sign, in lime-green neon, the sole monitor of my ebbing existence.

Burgerama. Blank. Burgerama. Blank. Burgerama. Blank. Blank.

Sally Pomme Clayton

Erotocritos

Erotocritos sang under the balcony
the balcony of Aretousa
Princess Aretousa.
He was just a poet
a balladeer
making songs and rhymes.
But his voice
his words
played against her skin.
She listened and she loved.
And she longed for darkness
to sit in the shadow of her window
and open her dress
so that his words could touch her.

Eros had failed. His arrow hadn't pierced Tom's skin as deeply as Ada's. And now she was on a plane without him, misery clouding her. Going on holiday alone. Well, not a holiday. Research, she told herself. Searching out the myth of the Minotaur, King Minos'palace, and the labyrinth. She imagined wandering round Crete, stopping off at cafés, dreaming in the sun, sketching. A break from the 'what ifs'. The longing. The false hope of return. Perhaps she would finally accept the romance was over.

The plane was full of youths, gangs of boys looking as if they'd never been on a journey before. They cracked jokes, jostling, teasing, trying to out-do each other, but underneath they seemed afraid. Ada looked about. She was the only person travelling alone. She felt afraid too.

She closed her eyes and recalled the legend of the Minotaur. Half-man, half-bull, hidden in the labyrinth. Year after year, youths and maidens got lost in the maze of twisted passageways and were devoured by the beast. Then Theseus arrived, burnished and bold. Ariadne's heart leapt. She followed him with big eyes and gave him her ball of thread. Theseus slew the Minotaur and the thread guided him out of the labyrinth. As he stepped into the cheering crowds, Ariadne ran towards him, her face shining with anticipation, and Theseus turned away. He abandoned her. Ada opened her eyes. The real beast of the story, she murmured, looking out of the window and thinking of Tom.

> *How could Aretousa tell him*
> *her secret response?*
> *One night she reached for the fruit bowl*
> *took an apple*
> *kissed its rosy flesh*
> *and threw it down.*
> *Erotocritos pressed it to*
> *his cheek and chest*
> *put it in his pocket*
> *vowed to keep it until he died.*
> *But he was just a poet*
> *a balladeer*
> *how could he marry a King's daughter?*

Ada arrived at the site early. The paths were being washed and the cool of the morning remained. She hoped to find some trace of the labyrinth. Knossos would have been elegant, marble staircases, corridors with light-wells, storehouses for oil and wine, channels for water. Ada stared: there was concrete everywhere, blurring into the original stone floors, filling in broken edges, squaring off walls and window ledges, patching up pots. And the frescoes she had looked at so many times in the library had been painted over. Occasionally she found a grinding dish or water tub that hadn't been reconstructed. Whatever had been here was buried under an archaeologist's fantasy. Arthur Evans had eradicated Knossos and built his own myth.

Ada felt dizzy. She lay on a slab of stone in the shade of a pine tree. Drops of pine resin had splashed onto the ground. She rolled some between her fingers and sniffed it. She drifted into sleep with the sound of the cicadas, their chorus increasing in volume and pitch, building to a deafening crescendo, then suddenly falling silent, and just as suddenly starting up again. When she woke, a hawk was fluttering above the tree. Ada wondered if it descended from a family of hawks who had always lived there, stretching back to Minoan times, keeping the real secrets of the past.

She walked back along the road to catch the bus, past stands selling Fanta and plaster copies of goddesses wound round with snakes. Perhaps the labyrinth had never been here.

She wanted it badly, nearly as badly as Evans. Well, a King lived here, she consoled herself, and he might have had a daughter whose heart was broken.

At the tournament for Aretousa's hand
Erotocritos was swift.
She watched
willing him on.
Just behind him always
was the Prince of Byzantium
heavy with jewels.
Erotocritos won all the challenges.
Aretousa's father took the hand of Byzantium
and with his eyes on a grand future
on Byzantium's glittering shores
bordered with marble palaces,
gave it to Aretousa.

Walking along beaches as a shortcut never works. Ada carried her sandals and splashed through the water. It looked like a straight line along the beach and back to town, but as she walked, gullies appeared, and cliffs jutted out. A huge half-built stadium didn't get any closer. She passed a fisherman and asked how long it would take to walk back.

"Ena ora?" One hour?

"Mia ora," he answered, and gestured to his van parked up on the beach, suggesting she come with him. Mia ora – only half an hour.

Ada waved and smiled; she was fine to walk.

Afterwards, she discovered that mia is the feminine for one, one feminine hour. It was her hour and she was travelling it. One feminine hour later, she was struggling. The curving lines of the harbour seemed further away. The sand looked flat and smooth from a distance but gave way under her feet, sea water filling her footprints, the sand turning to shingle, collapsing with each step. She kept going, aiming for the stadium, but she never reached it. The beach turned into a rubbish dump and ended abruptly, as a river pushed out into the bay.

She put on her sandals and turned into a wasteland of broken cars and warehouses. Men looked up, wondering what she was doing. She climbed up to the road. It was a motorway with no pavement. Lorries rumbled by; jeeps and open-top holiday cars raced past. Ada strode along trying to look purposeful. She passed a wayside shrine covered in dust and crossed herself swiftly. The road bent away from the shore and back again. Thin pavements appeared and disappeared. She followed them, crossing from one side of the road to the other. Ada pushed herself on. She wasn't lost – just round this corner, and the next, and the next. The town appeared, but nothing changed – the same derelict buildings, dust-covered cars, piles of rubble. The road bent back to the shore. At last, the flag on the fort broke over the skyline. Ada turned into the hotel.

Aretousa flung herself on the ground.
Never never
it was impossible.
She begged for Erotocritos
but he was just a poet
a balladeer.
Her father
stood over her,
sliced off her long golden hair.
"If you won't marry who I want you to marry
you won't marry at all."
And shorn like a nun,

she was pushed
into a tower.
A dark tower.

Giorgos, the owner of the hotel, did everything, serving behind the bar, cooking, cleaning. Ada sat by the bar, reluctant to go out. Giorgos pushed a table next to the window to catch some breeze, and spread it with a paper cloth.

"Join us, Adaa," he said, stressing the last syllable of her name.

His friend Kostas arrived, carrying a dish piled with grilled fish. "I was fishing – fresh today."

They ate it with juicy tomato salad, dunking rusks into the bowl and leaving them to soak up the juice.

Ada was grateful. She didn't feel strong enough to face the loud, "Ena!" One! from the waiter, as he steered her to a dark corner, placed a basket of the oldest, most dried-up bread before her, where she would sit, conspicuously one, among couples and families.

Giorgos and Kostas told jokes about the people from Anogia, dreadful jokes that made Anogians the fools of Crete. They were the same jokes rehashed and relocated all over the world. Ada didn't care; she sipped musty raki and laughed with them. Giorgos split open some figs.

"Did you grow them?" asked Ada.

"No, we stole them," Giorgos laughed. "Well, no Greek likes to have a fig tree in their garden. Have you seen them? Those trees are ugly! So we plant them outside the village and then we go and steal them! Anyway, what are you doing here on your own Adaa? Looking for men?"

"I'm looking for a story."

"Okhi! Impossible. You must be looking for a husband. I was in love with an English girl once. After one year, she told me I was Westernised. She made me the way she liked me. Then she left me. Later I married a girl much younger than me, and now we are divorced. I guess I was the one who was immature. I feel badly I got divorced. When I was a child, it was never in my mind that I might divorce. In those days, women served men, looking after everything – the children, the house, the money. And the men went to the kafenio. It was nice for them. Why should they give it up? Now it is different. I do it all, and have no time to take care of myself. I put on weight, no one will want me. People think they will be happy with more freedom, but I don't know."

No one spoke. For a moment, Ada felt lost inside a great, tangled-up web. She didn't know where to stand. Then they burst into laughter. They laughed and laughed. And Ada rubbed her eyes with a paper serviette.

"If you want stories, Adaa," said Giorgos, "go into the mountains."

The tower was surrounded by guards.
Aretousa's father raged
"Stay there
for three years
until you learn obedience."
And the entrance of the tower
was walled up.
Inside, it was damp and dark.
There were baskets of bread
barrels of water
boxes of candles.
Aretousa
prayed and sang
walked about briskly to keep warm
made a bed on the rough floor
lit one candle to the next
and dreamt about Erotocritos.
Her poet
her balladeer.

The buses were anarchic, shifting their doors temperamentally. Sometimes doors opened at the front, sometimes the side, sometimes the back. Ada missed several buses waiting at the wrong door. Even Cretans hovered around the buses uncertainly, wondering which door would open.

Ada went to a stall near the bus stop and her ticket was pushed through a tiny hole in a window. When the bus arrived, she leapt on, dropping things in a disorganised way. It was either fifteen minutes early or thirty minutes late – probably both. The bus wound its way up into the hills, past olives and olives and olives. The ground was burnt yellow and brown. They climbed higher and higher, the air cooling. Ada closed her eyes at the sheer bits and joined the old women who crossed themselves as they passed a car crash on a twisty bend. One by one, people got off and the bus stopped outside a factory.

"End of journey," said the driver, rolling a cigarette.

"But I can't get off here," cried Ada.

The driver laughed. "Ok, I take you back."

He dropped her in the middle of nowhere. "Other side," he said, waving his hand casually and driving away.

Ada put down her rucksack. She was high up, overlooking a wide plain. Above her, barren crumbling rock. She heard a faint jingling sound. She looked about – perhaps they put bells in the trees? But the bells grew louder, and she was suddenly surrounded by a great crowd of bleating and pushing goats with bells round their necks. One goat, with horns and a huge bell, leapt onto a rock to watch as the flock passed. Behind them came a young man wearing jeans and holding a shepherd's crook. He was singing a repeating cycle of phrases that sounded almost like speaking. He waved his crook at Ada, then disappeared round the corner, with his song.

* * * *

"Frapeh meh gala i zakhari!" smiled the old woman, placing a long glass on the table. Ada repeated the words and the woman nodded. "Kala." Good. Ada sank into her chair, engulfed in a haze of bright pink bougainvillaea. The sound of teaspoons tinkling against glass, clacking rosaries, whistles, shouts of "Neh!" Yes! floated across the square. Outside the kafenio, the old men sat, with gentle wrinkled faces and kind eyes, playing cards in the shade. A young woman appeared and put a dish of ice-cold grapes before Ada.

"Our grapes," she said.

"The shepherds," asked Ada, "what do they sing?"

"Erotocritos. They sing Erotocritos. A love story. It belongs to Crete."

Three years slowly passed.
Aretousa waited for the sound of hammer on stone
waited for her father to set her free.
But she did not hear the sound of hammer on stone.
Her father had forgotten her.
Aretousa took the bread knife
and scratched at the wall,
scratching and scraping
until her arms ached
until her hands were red raw
until she had made a tiny hole.
She peered out.
The ground was burnt, black and bare
fires smouldering
buildings in ruins.
The kingdom was a wasteland.

Father and son rested lyres on their knees, drew bows across the strings, and began to sing Erotocritos, their voices soft and rough, their playing crazy and tender. Ada sat in the front, entranced. Suddenly, the father put down his lyre and a row broke out. The son exploded, shouting, banging. The wives and daughters retreated onto the dark street, taking Ada with them.

"Men drink too much raki," they laughed. "It happens nearly every night." These men were fighters. Resistance was their history; they couldn't find another way.

"But their music is good," said Ada.

"Woman is always second," tutted the son's wife. "I only survive by prayer and friends."

One of the uncles put his arm round her waist. "Women rule from behind the curtain," he grinned.

They wandered through the narrow streets, found a bar and drank lemon tea. Ada asked about Erotocritos.

"It's passed down. Shepherds learn it. Some old men on the hillside know all ten thousand verses. They are real poets, improvising with the fifteen syllable line. When the young ones get good, they sing under the window of their sweetheart. When they really fall in love, they go up to that rock, high up outside the village, and sing, so the whole neighbourhood hears. Then everyone knows there will be a wedding."

* * * *

Ada searched for Zeus' cave. The rock that Cyclops threw at Odysseus. The temple of Artemis. There were stories everywhere. But her heart wasn't in it. There were couples everywhere, and she missed Tom.

"Want a boyfriend?" winked a waiter.

"For your husband?" asked an old woman selling fruit.

Ada felt foolish. She'd imagined it would be different. Oh, romance. She wished she could stop living in stories.

Aretousa crawled out of the tower
picked her way
across rubble and bodies.
The palace was a ruin,
her father killed
the city invaded by Byzantium.
She went into the hills.
Whole villages hid in caves
their spirits unbreakable,
women making food from ragged herbs
men descending to the towns in gangs to fight.
An army of resisters joined them.
Among the rebel soldiers,
Erotocritos in disguise.

"Don't fight the waves," said Irini. Ada splashed and gulped, and her eyes stung with salt. Irini bobbed next to her. Afterwards they spread towels on the sand and lay on their stomachs.

"I was in Manchester, in a pub. All night long, guys brushed up against me. I was so shocked; they were touching me, a village girl from Crete! If my father knew, he'd be horrified. I've never even had a boyfriend."

"Never?" asked Ada.

"It has to be someone the family chooses. Really, I want to work as a translator, but I can't leave my family. They've given me so much; I have to help them."

Ada hugged Irini and promised to write. As the bus pulled away, she felt her freedom, and was ashamed and relieved. Retaining Erotocritos came with restrictions. Ada wondered what she gained and lost.

"I'm a journalist," she lied to the man sitting next to her. He nodded – that's why a girl would travel alone. The bus wound its way to the coast, past a strip of resorts. Ada remembered the boys on the plane; she hadn't seen them. They had gone to a resort and stayed there.

* * * *

By midnight the bar was packed. The lyre player whipped the audience into a frenzy and they began to dance. A group of older women pulled Ada onto her feet. It was a 12-step dance, but she could only find two steps. Her feet clumsy in sandals, her dress billowing, flushed and breathless, she tried to keep up with the women in their dainty heels and slim-fitted trousers. Ada's head bent, she stared at their feet, trying to copy their steps. The circle shifted. They linked hands, dropped, and linked again. Ada found herself moving round the circle. For a moment, she gave up – escaping, searching, getting lost, holding on, letting go. Suddenly she found she was dancing. And there was freedom. For a few moments, Ada was dancing all the steps. She looked about in utter joy. She was dancing and she could feel the pattern of the dance. It wove in and out, like a labyrinth. She was the labyrinth, and she was dancing it.

Blood was shed
much blood was shed
before the enemy left their shores.
Then Erotocritos removed his disguise
and went to Aretousa.
He rolled an apple at her feet
and sang.
His words touched her.
Her dress fell open
and her hair grew.
It was her poet
her balladeer.
Erotocritos sang
sang so the whole neighbourhood would hear.
Then there was a wedding.
A wedding, oh a wedding.
Such a wedding.

Ada's plane was delayed. She scoured the few shops and found a battered, expensive translation of Erotocritos. She propped it up on her knees while she ate the sweaty food provided by the airline. She had been looking for one story and found another. Every day had been like that.

The book linked the 15th century Cretan poem to an Italian translation of a medieval French romance that was similar to a Middle Eastern epic. Ada laughed. Crete was the labyrinth, twisting away and turning toward itself.

The gangs of boys filled the plane. Subdued and sunburned, they fell asleep instantly. Ada joined them, dreaming of broken bits of pottery. When they landed, she got a text from Tom saying he'd found work in America. Ada breathed out. Just for a moment, it seemed easier to let Eros go.

Samantha Coerbell

Spider on My Wall

Oh, spider on my wall
why don't you ever crawl?
could it maybe be
that you are as lazy as me?
is your little spider life
turned topsy turvy?
day after day you remain
shadow glinted figure,
are you stuck in the blue of my wall?
hiding from your colony?
has your spider boyfriend
sucked the life out of you
that in some sick way you
don't even want to move
until he brings his sorry
8-legged arachnid spinneret
back to shoot a little extra
webbing over you
you told him you weren't into that kinky shit
bondage wasn't your scene
the pink pussy cat scared you
but he wrapped four of his legs around you
and made all sorts of promises
shot a spiel that spiraled around your abdomen
the warmth was nice until
he cut the silky web he wound
and crawled away
leaving you
»

feeling
cozy and alone
until you realized
cozy
was a dumb feeling
you were just alone
For months you've been on my wall
patiently waiting for him
to die
eating away at your own flesh
while you know
he's at the biggest dead fly on the block
sucking blood with the fellas
tellin' em' what a thick web he can weave
how all the queens be breaking
3 o' they legs
to do the horizontal crawl with him
'bout the 1000s of eggs he got
that goin' look just like him
can he spin a tale?
can he?
the wall doesn't want anything from you
legs 'most gone
moving on with your existence
would only rip at the image you once had of yourself
as a full spider
with the ability to trap and suck fo' yo' damn self

Oh, spider on my wall
I leave you to yourself
because to try to move you
would mean I had something better to offer
like I'm in a position to give advice
spider, sweetie,
I only got these two legs.

Samantha Coerbell

I Think Air

Tasting your words is mesmerizing.
I listen to the smile on your face
delighted at what I have made.
Craftsperson of a kind of madness.
Designing delirium
out of the fabric of our lives.
100% cotton-mouthed
at your touch.
99.9% purely enthralled
at every decibel that ripples
over my skin.
My 2000 parts are calling for you.
Even now.

We delude ourselves
that a weekend is enough time.

I dream of kissing you
and don't even wait 'til I'm asleep.
Can I call you with champagne in me?
Drunk from wanting,
wanting to be drunk by you.
Taken by mouth,
sipped and swallowed over time
my body a bottle-full broken on the bow
of two ships that passed in a
Mississippi night.

Rowan Oak is a regret almost.
How would it have been if we had kissed there?   »

if your good sense did not hinder you,
if I was bold enough to lick your teeth.
What would we be capable of now?

This is disturbing
on so many levels.
I can't get off the first floor
and the next level is sky.
I think air will support us,
wrap and cradle us
as we dance toward some destiny
built of curiosity and compassion.

We're running out of excuses.
I want to lose my breath,
staring at the precious
beauty of your eyes
picking your brain and
sifting my fingers in you
plumbing our depths
until we are
exhilarated beyond anticipation

I can't breathe straight.

Merle Collins
Island Myth: Once, on an Island

Once, on an island,
were people who lived in the mountain, and feared the distant sea
and those who roamed by the sea, ashamed of the remote mountain.

Mountain stories warned
that sea was a wild wet place, with a sound like thunder,
with no branches, that in the sea there's nothing to hold if you fall.

Sea stories warned
that mountain was a dangerous place, always dark, always the
    sound of thunder,
that in the mountain you're attacked by branches and brambles.

And so they lived,
free and wild in the roaming blue,
free and wild in the verdant green.

Mountain never strayed from its heights
but sea, bold blue roamer, licked at mountain's foundation, eroded,
murmured that mountain tasted of danger, mysterious.

And mountain children, angry at sea's roaming erosion,
went in search of sea, set off a sleeping volcano,
caused a great conflagration.

Sea children, angry and vengeful, roamed to seek that murderous mountain
and so they reached what they thought a wild place, dark, mysterious,
thunder of drums in crescendo, costumed people, food floating in trays
    on still water.   »

Rushing from the bushes, they cut down baskets of food, captured
thundering drums and retreated, rejoicing, for their world,
they thought, was a safer place, now they had struck against evil.

But when they went home rejoicing, the elders wept and tore at their garments,
Lamenting, saying you were still in the valley, you hadn't reached the
	mountain,
and they made offerings of peace, fearing the hook and the bit

knowing that today for policeman, tomorrow for thief,
and then, there were island stories, for the island became a dangerous place,
always the sound of thundering waves, always the noose of branches and
	brambles,

always the tramp of policemen, and forever the whisper of thieves.

Patric Cunnane

Baltimore

In the lonely city I reach out to you
Twin souls buried in darkness and light
We are the poor offspring of our dreams
Watching snow drift across Baltimore skies

In the lonely city our fingers touch
An electric connection distributing
Power to all circuits. In your eyes
I see a door opening, reflecting a second door
Leading to a corridor of hope

In the lonely city you reach out to me
It is such a simple thing –
One human being
Moving toward another

The Baltimore traffic backs up for the weekend
Friday's snow forms a cushion between our lips
Our warm breath gives winter notice
We are reaching out across this city, circling like ships

Patric Cunnane
Café Paradiso

Cork City gulps April sunshine
The air that refreshes after winter
We gulp red wine in Café Paradiso
Learning new words for love

Your beauty is a thing of wonder
I never knew your loveliness before
You open your heart to me
I walk through its lonely door

A parentless child in Belfast
A child at war in a city at war
Longing for love and star-filled nights
In a city landscape spelling NO

You tell me of your lovely daughter
Rachel, how you chose her name
You tell me of your husband
Your cottage, the things that keep you sane

We have one more glass
Then one glass more
And another glass to be really sure
When we leave Café Paradiso
The world will care a little more

Fred D'Aguiar

Letter from King Ferdinand of Spain to the Tainos in October 1493

My wife waits for me
in our unmade bed. She bruises
easily against my bones.
We fit together when I see fit.
She leaves me with an ache
not there when I approach her
nameless, no date in mind,
my bones fitted to a spine curved
by time, time and again by a ring
a ring and a ding dong.

Icy bones in my bony bed,
not mine alone, more yours
than mine. Bones scrambled,
a hieroglyphics lost to me now
in my coupling with history, curled
here beside me in a fitful sleep
typical of a body without blame,
yet one full of dreams. You see
or refuse to see that history,
with a hey and a ho and a lo,

is my mistress. I am in a bed
made for bones sweetened
with milk and rice, milk turned
by time, a grain of rice for each   »

second we share. History with nothing
lying beside it but my silly bones
pared of flesh, bones unshackled,
bones that mark time, porous time,
and more of the same
in the same old same old.

Joolz Denby
Trouble

I live in Bradford. It's a stone-built city in the North of England, crouched in a wide valley like a refugee finding safe haven. Above us, as we plod round town or stumble down the Leeds Road, the skies unfurl like tattered banners: blue, concealing, cloud-embroidered. Once it was a wealthy place, very wealthy; great families made fortunes from woollen cloth. They built monuments to their beloved money; rearing sandstone palaces crusted over with decorative carving as thick as the family Bibles that recorded their lives. In Gothic niches, blind, craggy saints and kings stare into the grey; adamantine queens and petrified sailing ships stud fretted facades; ropes and swags of deathless ivy and acanthus drape and festoon in perpetual glory; the stone rendered almost liquid by the mason's skill.

The money's gone now. It's been gone a long time and now the city rags along in an unravelling tatter of poverty. We live here; we eat sag aloo and peshwari naan, and drink thick, yellow mango lassi at midnight in basement curry houses. If we need fresh air, we go to the moors and clamber round the gritstone crags that punch up from the earth like fists and mirror in nature those buildings we walk past every day. The city still hides itself, a strange place no stranger knows, cloaked in a scruffy pall of Sixties town planning. It's a crazy stone puzzle, an empty castle, decayed and abandoned, inhabited now only by squabbling tribes who build camp fires in the big hall at night, to keep off devils and the terrible stars.

Just out of the Town centre are the tall, slab-fronted mills, long abandoned by the clattering looms or whirling spindles. A couple of these have been colonised by musicians looking for a place to make noise all night without the neighbours ringing the coppers. We've got a studio in one of these hives; a room facing out on the long road heading to the country; but there's nothing rural here. It's where the prostitutes work, since the vigilantes drove them out of Manningham. It's a dark canyon of six-storey ex-industrial nowhere, it's got a hundred nooks and ginnels, alleys and dead ends, and in winter, it's witchy cold and the rain drives in sideways sheets, as the wind tumbles a scurfy scum of rubbish along the pavements and slaps old plastic bags and crisp packets round the girls' skinny ankles.

Up and down, they walk, all night long. At three in the morning when, they say, the dying give up the ghost, they suck off punters in parked cars or shuffle from foot to foot, waiting and hoping, their pinched faces pushing out of the dark, pallid as blisters. The cars slow down, the newer girls hastily stitch an imitation of a smile onto their icy faces because the punters like it if you smile and say, "looking for business, love?" in a bright way; it makes them feel the whole deal is a bit personal, a bit tart-with-a-heart-of-gold. The more experienced girls can't be bothered with all the fake chumminess, it's too much effort, and it's much easier to fuck someone you loathe than smile at them. Not that the punters know that, not really. I don't know what the punters actually think, if they think at all – but if they think the girls like them, or like sex, or like their lives, God help them, because it's a fool with his foot on the road to Hell who lives in blind ignorance of that kind of truth.

If a punter wants something more adventurous than can be done easily in a vehicle, they'll take him to a bit of waste ground across the road from our building. Amongst the woody thickets of buddleia and Japanese knotweed, there's a bit of plastic sheeting thrown over a couple of pallets, garnished with an old sofa cushion bursting it's filthy raggled guts from weather and damp. There the girls do what they do; in the mouldy stink, in the rain, in the bone-scraping frost, for a tenner or maybe even for twenty, if they don't use a condom. Then when the punter shuffles off they jack up, or smoke, or if they're very new, cry.

The girls have learnt that our building is used by musicians, and stopped bothering with the patter when the lads pull up in their beaten-up wreckers. If anything, they've got used to seeing us loading and unloading music gear at odd hours and getting on the tour bus, or working through until dawn. Now they wave, sometimes, or beg for fags, or lifts up to the gas station, or tell the lads if they've left the car lights on, or tap them for a few pence if it's a slow night. It's a kind of truce; not friendship, not like we're mates or anything. It's just that we're not straight, not from the straight world – we're not in the Life, but we're not social workers, or citizens, do-gooders, reporters or punters. So we balance on the blade's edge – uneasy allies in an invisible war. It's a delicate kind of peace, though, always just a breath away from trouble.

And trouble always comes, whether you like it or not.

Our building isn't finished; the conversion to studios and rehearsal rooms costs money and the weasely hippie who master-minds this warren constantly runs out of cash. Sometimes he has all-night bongo parties or gigs on the ground floor. This, plus the fact he's daubed the rotting brick with day-glo murals has led to the belief in that wannabe London, Leeds, that Bradford is covertly harbouring a genuine, authentic underground music scene. Well, that's as maybe, as they say round here. So anyhow, after the über-hippie has a rent party, he does some building work. This is carried out mainly by Steve.

You'd never notice Steve in a crowd. You'd never give him a second glance. He's a short, silent, thin bloke in his late forties; an ex-drop-out from the Seventies. He wears ancient Lennon specs with bottle-bottom lenses so greasy and fingerprinted I'm surprised he can see out of them, knackered old work clothes, and his straggle of mousy hair is slipping slowly backwards. He's a no-colour person, if you know what I mean – sometimes, if the light's right, he almost seems transparent. But he's an excellent carpenter, and he lives in that enclave of pot-heads who so successfully drove the junkies out of their street and now exist in a kind of semi-legal herb heaven. Steve has seen a bit of life; he's had his share of knocks, he likes to say when you can coax a word out of him, but now he's got a family, kids; he's OK – and behind the opaque lenses, his sky-blue Northern eyes flicker with love.

Oh, one thing I may not have mentioned is that the prostitutes round by the studio are children. Not one of them is over sixteen and some of them are twelve or thirteen. They are not the feisty, seasoned pros of legend who may, or may not, exist outside the popular press and TV dramas. These girls are just that – girls. Most are drug addicts or alchies, or both. They're ruined by the savagery of their brief infancies and they're riddled with diseases ranging from chlamydia and clap, through to multiple-drug-resistant syphilis and AIDS. Some of them have PID, some TB. Some of them know they're dying. Cold sores tattoo their rosy, unformed mouths and their eyes are black jelly. They wear tight, imitation clubwear market stall fashions and never wash their make-up off, just add more layers until it forms a cacky mask. They shake a lot and their minds are shot by what they've known and smelt and seen and done, so straight folk often think they're thick.

The girl, I'll call Marie, was in better shape than some. She was mixed race; her freckles stood out like paint splatter under the harsh sodium street light. She always wore her fluffy, tea-coloured hair scraped back with gel into a pony tail that exploded into curls and was pulled so tight it lifted the corners of her long, storm-grey eyes. She usually wore a silver puffa jacket, so she stuck out a bit from the others. But she looked as if she ate, she didn't chain-smoke but chewed gum instead, and her gaze was still fairly level and engaged. There was some life left in her face. One night, as we drove away from the studio, we saw her playing hopscotch to pass the time: one, two, one, two, turn on one leg. She was concentrating, her tongue stuck out a little, her forehead creased. Tall for her age, a gawky thirteen year-old all knees and bony wrists; leggy, like an unbroken colt.

Watching her drove Steve mad. He couldn't bear it. She reminded him, he said, of his eldest daughter. He couldn't stand to think of what that little lass did at night – what all those little lasses did – when his girl was tucked up safe in bed at home. It wasn't right. It wasn't fair. What was wrong with a world that could let this happen? He could only talk in clichés, not being a speaking type of man, but his words were strong because they were true and truth, Steve thought, would prevail, as would justice. His anger burnt slow and steady, brooding banked under his good hippie hatred of violence and conflict and all that chunter about sex workers and prostitute's unions the women's groups his partner belonged to favoured. His fury made me feel guilty; more than guilty, ashamed. The anger I'd felt when we first set up in the building and I'd seen the age of the girls and their life, had been eaten away by the everyday-ness of the whole thing. I'd got used to seeing the girls. I'd got used to making my excuses about there being nothing I could do, to not thinking about it. His anger was fresh, it was re-born every dawn, it was wick and pure. It turned and coiled and twisted in him like a fiery serpent biting its own tail. It wouldn't go away.

Then, one night he was helping clear up after a gig downstairs, and as he took the rubbish out of the side door, he saw Marie's pimp's car pull up. Not a posh stretch limo. Not a sleek ebony Lexus or a silver BMW with a personal plate saying MACK 1. Just a ratty blue Cavalier with a bead cover on the driver's seat and a Magic Tree hanging from the rearview. And the pimp was no slouch-hatted, mink-coated, lover-lover man, diamonds in his gold teeth and one long fingernail to snort off. Marie's pimp looked like any big, heavy set, beer-bellied, out of shape bloke you'd see round town in TK Max or Burger King. He was bleary-eyed, stubble-chinned and wearing a footie shirt, shell trousers with Adidas up the side and a heavy gold Figaro chain. But Steve knew him, knew what he was. He'd seen him drop Marie off and pick her up, even seen her hand over the takings one night. And he lost it, he lost it big style.

Dropping the bulging black plastic bag, he strode towards the pimp, every inch of his slight body rigid with righteous ire. One of the lads who had been helping him clear up said at that point every-thing went into slow motion; the air turned to treacle. They started towards Steve, convinced he was going to get the living shit kicked out of him, but they weren't quick enough to grab him.

He stood in front of the big man, his head on a level with that winking gold chain, his bony, calloused finger prodding the guy's breastbone.

"You, you f-fuckin' bastard – you should f-fuckin' be ashamed of yersel – a little lass like that; I know what you are, you – you... I'm gonna..."

The pimp pulled back, a surprised look on his jowly face, then as he started to respond, a sliver blur launched itself from out of the shadows and Steve was shoved hard sideways, his glasses flying into the gutter.

"Get off my dad! You – get off my dad..."

Marie's shrill voice echoed through the narrow side street like a piece of shiny cloth tearing. Her father grabbed her by her pony tail and yanked her off Steve, spinning her round and shoving her into the road. Steve swayed, his face drained of blood, his myopic eyes blinking.

"That's yer – that's yer daughter? Fer fuck's sake – yer pimpin' yer own daughter?"

The big fella sneered, then laughed harshly. "Huh, yeah – an' what the fuck is it ter do wi' you, yer little fucker? It's my fuckin' kid, I can do what I like wi' her – it's none o' yer fuckin' business, right?"

Steve fell back, away from Marie's father, unable to think of any reply, unable to think at all. The big man copped a glance at the lads who were now tumbling through the door, tripping over rubbish bags and shouting Steve's name. Smacking a lone, four-eyed little nutter was one thing, dealing with four or five lads was another. He re-directed his irritation at Marie, shouting at her for causing him hassle and ordering her to get in the car. She folded herself into the passenger seat, her lower lip stuck out like a five year-old, and you didn't have to be a psychic to know she was saying it wasn't her fault, it wasn't, she didn't even know that bloke, honest.

They drove off.

The lads reached Steve as he was fumbling around for his specs. They comforted him as best they could; they got him a cuppa with loads of sugar and they sat with him while he drank it and wiped his eyes, long tremors shaking his legs as the adrenaline left his system. None of them knew what to say; nothing would make it all alright or make any real sense of the whole congealed mess.

Marie didn't come back to the road by our building, but none of us fooled ourselves she'd found salvation. There are plenty of other streets, and brothels, and saunas and portacabins on industrial deadlands where girls do fifty punters on a Saturday and have to piss in a bucket. Steve never talks about what happened, what he tried to do; he has turned back into himself and is quieter than ever, the brief blinding fire in his heart gone to ashes and cold cinders.

But I thought about it for a long time; and this is what I thought.

Love is both marvellous and terrible, we all know that; at least we do if we've lived past thirty. When it's marvellous – full of wonders and miracles – it's as blindingly beautiful as a great angel clothed in the gold of the undying sun; it's as breathtaking as nature and as small and powerful as a child's hand in yours. Love like this fills every cell of your body, it's honey-sweet, pure and without taint; it redeems and demands no return. It's truth and justice; it's hope and joy and it smiles like your beloved on a clean Spring morning; it's gentle, tender and not of the world.

And love is terrible; nothing is so terrible as bad love. It's not romantic or daring or glamorous, there's nothing good in it, nothing nourishing. When I think of it, I see the image of a card from an old French tarot pack I used to use when I was in the fortune-telling game. It's from the major arcana – the 'picture cards' my punters used to call them. The card is called 'Le Diable' – The Devil. It's one of the worst cards to get, really; I used to wince if anyone turned it up. On it, drawn in a crude woodcut style, is the Devil, standing on a little box or platform. He's not beautiful Lucifer, Son of the Morning, or some suave Satan in designer threads; he's sloppy fat, a brute, sweaty creature with a fuckwit smirk and leathery, vestigial wings. He's wearing nothing but some baggy leggings. His belly and tits push out bloated and coarse. In each of his blubbery hands is a leash, and attached to the leashes are a man and a woman. They're naked and on their mewling faces are expressions of horrible, unclean pleasure; they are gazing, twisted up and back, at the Devil, with deathless and immeasurable love in their brutalised eyes. They would do anything for their beloved master, and he knows it.

The meaning of the card is destruction, bondage, malevolence; it's violence, fatality, self-punishment and black magic. It's horror and it's the abyss; it's every foul thing, every humiliation, every scourge and every filthy degradation a human being can live through, and some they can't. Only when the card presents reversed is there hope, and then it's a long hard road back to the light.

Steve saw the Devil card that night, in Marie's father, in the vast, inherited ignorance of that man's daily, unthinking cruelty. He saw Marie, bound by bad love, by a terrible fate, to a father who used her child's passionate desire to love and be loved as a means to get money so he could buy himself beer, cigarettes and cheap gold jewellery.

And every little prostitute on that dark road does it for love; for the promise of love, for the flimsy and idiot illusion of love peddled to them by pimps and users; they suffer and they die, they are illuminated and they sacrifice everything, for the hope, just the hope, of love.

Oh, oh, beautiful and terrible; and everything for love.

* Trouble was commissioned as part of the PIMP performance project (2002), in which Apples & Snakes and Canongate Books asked eight artists to read Iceberg Slim's autobiography, Pimp, and respond to the work in any way they chose. The author asserts that this story has been drawn from real life; names have been changed to protect the innocent.

Denrele

Between Us

Last orders at the bar
six vodkas down and we're deep-talking
you're giving me your formula for world peace
I'm making a study of you, so I don't forget

You pose an argument
I counter it
tracing the outline of your face
with invisible fingers

You explain the error in my logic
I concur – grudgingly
noting the way your voice ranges
in tone and depth like a palette of blues

Do you know that
your eyes change colour
with your passions
paling and darkening like mood-stones

As we stand here trading opinions
only our words link hands
a bridge for distance neither you nor I
has tried to cross yet

In some other world, maybe
our lips have just met
and there's nothing between us
but intermingled breath

Michael Donaghy

Exile's End

You will do the very last thing.
Wait then for a noise in the chest,
between depth charge and gong,
like the seadoors slamming on the car deck.
Wait for the white noise and then cold astern.

Gaze down over the rim of the enormous lamp.
Observe the skilled frenzy of the physicians,
a nurse's bald patch, blood. These will blur,
as sure as you've forgotten the voices
of your childhood friends, or your toys.

Or, you may note with mild surprise,
your name. For the face they now cover
is a stranger's and it always has been.
Turn away. We commend you to the light,
Where all reliable accounts conclude.

Michael Donaghy

Southwesternmost

I've a pocketwatch for telling space,
a compass tooled for reckoning by time,
to search this quadrant between six and nine
for traces of her song, her scent, her face.
Come night, that we might seek her there, come soon,
come shade the southwest quarter of this chart,
the damaged chamber of my mother's heart.

Mare Serenitatis on the moon,
this blindspot, tearhaze, cinder in the eye,
this cloudy star when I look left and down,
this corner of the crest without a crown,
this treeless plain where she went home to die.
I almost hear it now and hold its shape,
the famine song she's humming in my sleep.

Claire Dowie

Tit Pincher, 1982

You wouldn't think you'd be likely to meet
a tit pincher in London
but you do. I did.
It was weird.
I was walking along, minding my business
wearing a t-shirt, even a bra.
(I was wearing a bra, but even if I wasn't
that isn't the point.)
It was summer.
It was weird.
He just walked over and grabbed my tit
and squeezed it, as bold as you like
and then said, "ooh!"
And I just stood there, horrified.
I should have punched him
but I didn't. I just stood there.
It was weird.
So the next day I went back to the spot
wearing a raincoat and specs for disguise.
Then I stood till he came
which he did. Then I pounced.
It was weird.
I just walked over and grabbed his balls
and squeezed them, as hard as I could
and then said, "ooh!"
And he just stood there, horrified,
going white and then red,
then he punched me
and I just lay there.
It was weird.

Stella Duffy
Silk Lovers

We haven't seen each other for over two years but we know what to do. We remember the rules. The promise. The vows of silk.

She has prepared herself for this moment. She wears a red silk camisole covered by lush black velvet and topped with sharp red lipstick. Her hair is long and newly dyed dark and covers the nape of her cool neck. She has readied both her own body and the room for his arrival. She has waited twenty-six months for him; she will not spoil this moment by even the most delicate scent of imperfection. There are red rose petals poured before the fireplace. The flames burn high and the petals will be dry before the night is over. The glasses of soft red wine are ready; there is a tiny table holding fingernail-size savouries and miniature cream chocolates.

When he arrives, he too is beautiful. Still too beautiful. Still more beautiful than her. He laughs, knowing how hard she has tried, knowing how easy it is for him. He has thrown himself together and, as always, his easy charm discomfits her. He has packed a small bag with all the tools they will need. The tools have not been used for over two years. Still, they are pristine and perfect. As he is.

A sip of wine, refuses chocolate, refuses food and then he is ready. She has no problem following his commands; they flow back like a catechism. He puts the handcuffs on her. They are made of thin paper, almost tissue but even more thin. And smooth.

"Don't rip them, now," he whispers.

She is led to the chair, her hands cuffed in her lap. Nearly naked.

I continued with the plan even though there was so much else to occupy my time. Watching you. Watching you with her. Watching you watching her. How could you forget to watch me?

She is so careful not to move, not to rip the tiny fibre threads that hold her hands together. The paper immobilises her more effectively than steel. It catches her breath as well as her skin. He places on the blindfold. It is made of thin silk, a single layer and white. Thin enough for her to see through.

She has seen through his deceit too. Though only after he showed it to her. Then it became transparent. She had not known where to look at first.

He undresses himself, to one side, where through the white silk his burnished bronze body is milk chocolate matte brown. He places scissors close by and stands the paper-cuffed woman in front of him. He takes the threads of silk - real silkworm silk they have been saving for this time – and slowly winds the threads between them. His feet to hers. Her legs to his. Their thighs to each other. Thousands of tiny worms died for this union. Each one softly ripped from its silk and re-laid in a fake cocoon of cotton wool so they could plait themselves together, solder their union.

I left the worms making their silk. I knew we would need it. Eventually.

She receives his body, silk of their skin wound round in silk. This is a winding not a wounding. Not yet. Two smooth bodies stretch, one up, one down to create face-to-face Siamese, twinning themselves in firelit melting. Paul hands her the scissors, which she holds in her softly cuffed hands. Her arms in front of him and in front of her, her bare arms and the stainless steel against the small swelling of her stomach. The tiny flesh swelling that warms and covers those eggs, holds safe her generations to come.

This shroud is softer even than the skin shroud I have lived in for two years.

There comes a point where the bodies are joined, his arms against her torso, their chests together. His free arms work above and behind her and now they wind their heads together, faces cheek to cheek. She sways, dizzy with looking into his eyes and breathing his breath and is gravity-held by his stronger passion.

He always said his was the stronger passion. Not a stronger skin though, I think.

This is not a thought I say out loud.

Now she and he are one, his arms free for a moment until he digs his thumbs, fingers, hands into and under the threads across her back. He is tied to her. She who is returned to him so they can do this thing. This thing they are committed to. This thing that will set him free of her longing, needing. Her disappointment. They spin. Twisting, four feet too close for purchase, rotating on the axis of what they have promised to do, what they bred the worms for, what she has promised to do.

Yes, I will. If you ever leave me, I will kill myself.

Promise?

I promise.

Good girl. Now go to sleep.

Difficult to move her hands, thin tissue cuffed inside the tiny convexed opening of their two stomachs, so gently to lift one hand above the other where the mingled running sweat has melted her paper bonds. She holds the criss-crossing steel blades and in the moment they fall, in the moment he goes, in the moment the steel meets the narrow resistance of skin and then a little sinew she finds herself worrying about the stain on the silk. The steel travels further in and catches – on an organ. Stomach? Spleen? A lung? She is not clear about the location of these secret parts. Both of them hear a small hiss but they do not know if it is his or hers. A hiss of escaping breath or hiss of escaping venom. They always were too close.

And she need not have bothered about the stains. She caught his blood herself. More full of blood than usual but not especially unpleasant.

When he left me I told him he really shouldn't.

His eyes were very near and she could see he was surprised. It was a look of horror and terror and sex and fucking and then bliss and then – nothing.

He was surprised by the steel, she was surprised by the nothing. She had expected more. Peace perhaps. Or a transcendental awareness. But no, he gave her nothing.

Typical.

She took the silk to a weaver and then to a dressmaker. The dressmaker made a thin band of cloth. Mary kept it. It would have made a lovely blindfold but that the red stains dried ochre and she could no longer see through it.

And there is no point in a blindfold that actually blinds.

You might as well close your eyes.

He did.

Helen East
The Trodden Path ⁘

This is the Path, the Trodden Path
earth, sand, ashes, water,
hills to desert to oceans edge,
past to future, birth to death,
from one great gateway to another
Birds united into one
wings woven all together
lift Laxshmi above the ground
carried in a cloud of feathers.

Over water, over earth
east to west, from dawn to dusk
from light to dark
from fire to frost
she nestles, feather bourne aloft.
Til day dying lower
   birds flying slower
sun sinking   rays shrinking
cold coming   wings numbing
sky blackening   strength slackening
night falling   birds calling
and now she falls too
down
like a stone.
frozen cold
to the bone
ears to tongue
head to toes.

»

Numb
still she goes on
seeking somewhere hope of a home.
Comes to an inn; frosty reception.
No warmth of welcome.
Yet she begs for a bite, a bed for the night
and grudgingly gets, then,
a corner, a crust.
Tastes like dust in her mouth
Now she waits on them,
the maid of all work,
all things thankless and hard.
Sleeps in a cellar,
eyes dimmed by the dark.
Silence enters her soul
cold numbs right to her heart.

This is the Path, the Trodden Path
memory of all that's passed.
East to West, dawn to dusk.
Silent stories in the dust.

* The Trodden Path is a narrative piece about journeys, actual and mythical, from the Indian subcontinent to England. It was performed with dance, music and simultaneous floor/path art. This extract relates the final journey and arrival in England of the heroine (Laxshmi), and combines the image of Goddess Laxshmi (on Garuda) with the true experiences of three women.

Zena Edwards

Blankets and Roses

for my mother

Watching Mama crochet
her concentration so profound and clear
seeing beyond the web and stitch
good times bad times play time hard times
moments of no time
walks to the water's edge of still lakes
the warm smell brown earth sun drying
after a rain fall when she tends her roses
patient silent cooking
deep fragrant bath soaks

Mama's face drops years when she crochets
the worry lines in her forehead lift
evaporate like malt whiskey on the tongue
her silvering hair catches the forty-watt
like glitter and a mirror ball
I see her back is straight now
Her shoulders loose
Her feet out of their shoes and her red nail polish sings out
fingers deftly magic up a multi-coloured world favoured by high purple

Mama crochets and I watch her
My Mama unfolds into a creation
spreading over her knees
onto the carpet across the floor
and into the street
blanketing the earth with her affection
her patience and her passion
I learn stillness

Zena Edwards

When the Leaves Have Fallen

When the leaves have fallen
And the trees are asleep
When the snow reflects
The sun
And the Winter Moon keeps
The city illuminated and iridescent in her pearly gaze
I'll treasure the sight of your breath
Escaping your lips
A delicate mist
And forever repeat the words that you uttered
Those silent dandelion puffs on the breeze of my memory

When the stars are extinguished
And the horizon is no more
My love for you will remain unpolished
    cherished

Lucy English

This Poem

This poem is six years-old.
Not finished.
Eating apples in the orchard.
Grass stains on my shorts.
I can climb the highest branches.
Touch the clouds with dirty fingers
And....

This poem is fifteen.
Sulky.
And written in purple pencil
In an exercise book kept inside a shoebox
At the back of the wardrobe.
Despairingly full of torment.
It's not fair. I have fat metaphors
And non-existent images.
I'm horribly, hideously, twistedly
Overwritten. Oh, so much pain!

This poem is thirty-five.
Mature.
An elegant sweep with a gilded pen.
An invitation to adultery.
I'll meet you in the car park at Waitrose.
It's all style and Carol Ann Duffy.
The strangest thing I ever stole was your ideas.

This poem is ancient.
Trotted out at picnics and weddings.   »

Still funny enough to make us smile.
Still poignant enough to make us hold back tears.
Oh, yes, we know this one.
"So long as men can breathe or eyes can see
So long lives this and this gives life to thee."

This poem is just born.
A high pitched wail
Of a wet idea.

Amy Evans

41 times

40 for free
39 for his sister
38 for his mother
37 for his baby
36 for the half-love at home
35 for the reasons he ran here instead of staying
34 there
33 for the soldiers who were on his trail
32 for the authorities who let him go
31 for the hours spent at the airport waiting
30 people in line
29 visas to go
28 denials
27 appeals
26 too few for hope
25 years-old, too young to die
24 dead anyway and many more to come
23 friends buried
22 burned alive
21 shot in cold blood and the rest got away
20 with major injuries and
19 maimed for life
18 who will never be able to multiply and make up for
17 year-old children with children of their own
16 chances missed
15 different times but choices are like that, impossible to guess that
14 could ever be a lucky number and
13 maybe he'll survive if he gets there in time   »

12 but this time too late
11 days without a minute of sleep
10 times punishment for doing the job no one else would
9 coffees to wash out
8 badly needed drinks
7 seconds to fall asleep and dream of Ricky Reel
and dream of Stephen Lawrence
and dream of Rodney King
and dream of Nigeria and what used to be home
and dream of the sound of footsteps coming up to the door
6 raps on the window or maybe
5 who'll ever know because
4 police officers' memories aren't enough to hold what's happened and
3 are failing failing
2 times would've kept him down but not far down enough for them
and let one of them be left for me
let one of them be left for me
leave me one don't let them
leave me out

Bernardine Evaristo

England, Oh My

Clouds of rouge on high-powdered cheeks,
Master of Ceremonies slinks on stage
in a goat's hair periwig and ship in full sail, as hat.
He is all afro-foppery.

"Welcome! *Willkomen*! *Bienvenue*!
to the Britannia Retrospective," he oozes at rows
of style-gurus, pens hovering over faux-zebra notepads.
"First off down the runway, amid flashing strobe

and 70s funk, is couture from the salons of Rome.
We have pink lurex togas, bubble-wrap helmets,
mink breastplates and psychedelic thongs,
evoking four centuries, ladies an' genl'men

when Latin was the spoken tongue
on these fair Celtic shores. Next we stumble
out of dry ice, clad in grey sacking, bi-furcated
for boys, belted for girls – the rustic look,

ideal for digging ditches and milking cows
in this 'ere this *Lundenwic*, this *Engla-lond*,
infused with Danes and Germans, creating
our Anglo-Saxon vibe. Watch out for the Vikings, though.

Rubber horns, PVC tunics, bloody perspex swords.
Check those wicked, beaded handbags
shaped like longships; have boat – will pillage,
a hint, methinks, of the plucking of African kora   »

with Elizabethan harp. Yes, a fine display
of chunky iron bracelets and necklaces, tattered culottes
(tie-dyed), tattooed backs. Slave-wear, ma'am, easy
to maintain and retrieve if stolen. Whooaah!

It's getting kinda tropical under this wig. Cue on
Victoriana's empire line. Sitar with damp pianola
accompany a ballet of tweed saris, tartan turbans,
whalebone bodices crushing shalwar kameez,

propelling us into a trance-dance finale
of 90s Jungle inspired by old colonial exports
and jewels returning to the crown.
A right show of big-batty leopard-skin bustles,

polka-dot yashmaks, grass stockings
and plumed cloth caps for all those johnny-just-comes
who've sailed to these shores since time
ever began... and so... under a solitary spotlight

...with a twirl and a flourish... I bow.
You've been a *fabulous* audience, I take off my hat to you.
Here! Catch it. Land ahoy and tutty byes.
(It is the ship we all came on, after all.)"

Dele Fatunla

Lagos Composition 1

Bursting at the seams,
Summer exploded into riots
We vaguely recognised as seeds
Of troubles;
Voices of hundreds sang as tear gas
Kissed their throats –
Our maid scurried to save us.
And to save themselves
Cars bore green leaves.
In the heat, something was growing,
Billowing into memories – from our
Balcony, muted politics floated,
Set to a running tap. Without knowing
We witnessed stillborn revolutions.

Dele Fatunla

Diaspora?

I am carved
In bold relief across
Your face.
You are standing like a shadow.
I am waiting to be the body.

Lawrence Ferlinghetti

Speak Out

And a vast paranoia sweeps across the land
And America turns the attack on its Twin Towers
Into the beginning of the Third World War
The war with the Third World

And the terrorists in Washington
Are shipping out the young men
To the killing fields again

And no one speaks

And they are rousting out
All the ones with turbans
And they are flushing out
All the strange immigrants

And they are shipping all the young men
To the killing fields again

And no one speaks

And when they come to round up
All the great writers and poets and painters
The National Endowment of the Arts of Complacency
Will not speak

While all the young men
Will be killing all the young men
In the killing fields again   »

So now is the time for you to speak
All you lovers of liberty
All you lovers of the pursuit of happiness
All you lovers and sleepers
Deep in your private dream
Now is the time for you to speak
O silent majority
Before they come for you

Lawrence Ferlinghetti

White Horse

Put the wine back in the bottle
Before the crystal glass is broken
The party is over
Goodbye
A new party has taken over
A new breed of men
as Henry Miller said
long time ago
A breed of barbarians
who didn't come through the gates
but grew up inside
They've made the White House
into a White Horse
their Trojan Horse
full of civilian soldiers
with weapons of crass destruction
which is a new name for their brains
or what might be diagnosed as
their pathological personalities
These masterminds
of the twenty-first century
and their Project for the New Century

And I heard the Learned Astronomer
tell the tale of the stars
in which the constellations conspired
to kill us all
out of pure hubris   »

and Territorial Imperative
since we were opposing
their total domination of the universe
And they hired these earthlings
in a White Horse
to do it for them

Lawrence Ferlinghetti

Brainwashed Poet

He dropped his pencil
And picked up a bomb
And the pencil writing backward
Came to a point
And exploded as if it were loaded
With something worse than verse
And he was the first poet
To have his pencil shots
Ring through the night
And such a success was he
That they named him
National Poet of the Plutocracy
Destroying our democracy

Ruth Forman

Play with Your Own Self

My happiness
does not depend on you
depends on me and me alone
so do not try to mold me like silly putty
imprint on me your cartoons of love
stretch me to a string of my patience
looking for a way to pull me apart
do not throw me on the floor
to see if I bounce
toss me to a friend to catch

I am not your play dough
do not cut me with stencils knives or cookie cutters
kneed blue or red or purple or green into my skin

I am not your play dough
not your silly putty
not the field for all your games

I am clay
mixed with the dust of the Old One and the waters of Yemaja
hold footprints of the ancestors
and seeds of those to come

if you forget I am ancient soil
you forget your own self
and where you come from   »

I am not a game
for your hands
to break mold or bounce
get over yourself
my happiness does not come from you or you
or you or you or you
I am not your game
if you must play
play with your own self.

Ruth Forman

Perhaps You're a Song

waiting to be whistled
tween some man's lips
perhaps you're a prayer
folded tween his hands
perhaps you're a love poem
waiting to be written

or perhaps you're already written
n wait
for someone to decipher your language

or perhaps you're not waiting
not waiting for anyone at all

perhaps you're already all of these things
a song a whistle a prayer a poem
playing just for the beauty of itself

Julian Fox

Denim Jacket

Yesterday I bought myself a denim jacket,
and for a while I felt quite happy
but when I got home I wasn't so sure
that it was the one that I actually wanted.
It felt much smaller, tighter than it had done in the shop
and there were no pockets either.
I asked a few friends what they thought about it,
and some did think that it looked a little small
but others thought that it was fine,
that it was supposed to look fitted.
I'll have to make up my own mind, I guess,
but I don't really like doing that.
Maybe I will take it back.

Mat Fraser

PIMP ✢

ICEBERG SLIM: paints a picture of punctures, of skin, those junctures of sin, at the crossroads of fate, every time choosing hate, yet you articulate, with a language that proves, how self-knowing the moves, masturbatory grooves, so this' the technique, to hook us as you speak, to our literariness, your language of finesse, as you found the way, to let us hear what you say, take the money we pay, for our consumptive lay, as you flex and inflect, you command our respect, for the way you're telling, is both vile and compelling, daubed with shit but you're smelling, of narrative pearls, gets the best of both worlds, as the story unfurls, of your 25 years, of blood hate and tears, caused by you and your fears, but so self-aware, cruel and debonair, with the language you're flaunting, zif you're transparently taunting, (the misogyny debases, comes in our faces), would it make the pain lighter, if you had a ghost writer, no the pimp never relents, just doubles the trick, making everything sick, paid for in the street, that's how you manage your meat, make a publisher's treat, get the money again, speak brutal truth then, recognising when, you've completed the wheel, with the verve and the zeal, of lifelong exploitation, of the system, the nation, that made your relation, into one of fear, now you got two careers, make everything clear, on a personal level, then the readership revel, in their Schadenfreude, who can read to avoid, unlike the bitch victims, of your predilections, all those inflections, were perfect reflections, of society's flailings, its needs and its cravings, but at the same time, charge you with the crime, mirrors held up, but Slim your cup, runneth over with wine, today's drugs more refined, did you pay your commission, to the girls you sent fishing, fair dues paid, to the women who laid, down to earn your wages, of sin and the pages, therein of your book, as from them you took, the last of their life, but Slim the tip, of this Iceberg's the quip, of the hustlin' ho dealer, but to the people that built, your empire, no guilt, for every penny you're taking, the money you're raking, from those many slaves, that you sunk into graves, gone from real deal inciter, to newly cherished writer, but while they're reading like fools, your story still has tools, to build them a memorial, to the primordial.

* Mat Fraser's piece is excerpted from a longer work commissioned as part of the PIMP performance project (2002), in which Apples & Snakes and Canongate Books asked eight artists to read Iceberg Slim's autobiography, Pimp, and respond to the work in any way they chose.

Chrissie Gittins

Driving in Adisa's Mercedes *

Automatic locking now manual,
mahogany abounds.
I sink into the seat
and am pulled through water.

The road's tide is made smooth
by immaculate suspension,
the bow stretches far into the swell.

We glide round eddies,
slide through spume,
until we reach the gilded shores of Colindale
and the Northern line,
which drags me home pell-mell.

* In July 2001 Apples & Snakes ran a project for secondary schools at
the RAF Museum, Hendon. Several schools came together to work with
poets using the massive historic aircraft in the museum as a starting
point. Before the workshop/ performance day, the poets met at one of the
schools involved to get to know one another and talk about ideas. I'd
never met my fellow poets before and it was an interesting interlude –
we read/performed to each other and ate good biscuits. After the meeting,
Adisa gave me a lift back to Colindale tube station in his 'new' car.

Chrissie Gittins

How to Make a Cup of Tea

for William Patten School, Stoke Newington, London

Take the mouse out of the teapot.
Pour in two cupfuls of ice.

Boil the kettle and leave the water to cool.
Find some tea.
This could be elephant and magnet tea,
hundreds and thousands tea,
or – the always popular – bag of nails tea.

Shovel the tea into the pot.
Don't bother pouring out the iced water –
it will mingle nicely with the cool water from the kettle.
Pour the water from the kettle steadily into the teapot.
Leave it for half an hour to settle down and stop giggling.

Find six teacups. Six is always a good number.
Don't worry about the saucers.
Never make the mistake of asking if anyone takes sugar.
If they say "Yes" and you've run out,
then you'll have to go out and buy some.

Milk the cat.
Bake a cake.

Martin Glynn

I AM

I AM .....
Not invincible ....
I AM ....
Not capable of stopping a bullet
With my chest
I AM
Not strong enough to prevent the
Flow of tears from my tired eyes
I AM
No longer able to cover up my mistakes
With lies and deceit
I AM
No longer capable of hiding my fears
As they are too visible
I AM
Not dealing too well with my
Your ....
Our ....
past
I AM

Struggling with the changes I know I must make
I feel ... I AM
Bleeding
   Crying
      And hurting inside
         Struggling to maintain my focus
           I AM ..... Too hard on myself   »

I know ..... I AM
Bursting at the seams
In a transitional phase
At a new place
At a crossroads
In a world of confused memories, pain, and
Nostalgia
But !!!!!!!!
I am
Crying
Releasing tears for the first time
No longer scared of the confrontation
Not afraid of the fears
BECAUSE
I
AM
No longer caught up in the
Bullshit .. pretence .. bullshit ... pretence Bullshit .. pretence ...
bullshit pretence Pretence .... Bullshit ... pretence ... bullshit

WHY?

Because I AM
Me
I AM
No longer tied to you
Goodbye Dad ..

Goodbye ......

I AM free
I AM free at last
I AM free to choose
I AM free to invest in myself
I am free

Salena Saliva Godden

Fierce Pink Lamb-Chop

You don't return my calls,
But you keep my packages and proposals.
You don't e-mail me,
And it eats at me.
It's making me paranoid,
Feel worthless.
You are either simply rude,
Or busy – Or both.
And I am eager and enthusiastic and too ambitious.
But if I was a boy,
And if we were talking Techno,
I'd be a DJ,
And you would need me to keep your finger on the pulse,
The beat, as you are ageing and thinning and fatting.
And I'd remind you of you
When you were young,
With dreams and spunk.

You'd see me as being a bit of a lad
With potential and drive,
Which I am,
Except I am a girl and you don't return my calls,
My e-mails and it eats at me.
It's so damn irritating.
You are definitely and positively rude,
You are absolutely busy,
You are probably very busy and very rude
Very rude and very busy and very rude and busy
And gay,
Possibly probably gay.   »

Otherwise you'd let me pitch this to you face to face,
Over coffee or a pint,
Or over dinner,
Or even over breakfast… or perhaps not.

If I was a boy you would meet me and we'd talk about football,
How we might both actually dislike it,
And tits, we'd talk about Playstation and tits.
We would talk about Lara Croft's tits.
We'd talk about *Lord of the Rings* the movie.
And we'd both love that Nick Hornby book,
Ibiza benders and Thai prostitutes, and
How your uncle sucked out a snake bite once,
And hot-sweat chilli-laced curry recipes,
Police car chases, violent vomit, Elvis and
Drunken tales of losing your house keys,
And accidentally climbing in the wrong window, the neighbour's window,
To wake up and terrify your sexy girl neighbour who'd been sleeping.

But alas, I am just a mere pale pink lamb-chop,
A soft underbelly, boob-wobbly, arse-shaker,
Lavender-sniffing, essentially oily candle-burning,
Wearer of pretty glass beads and tights and mascara,
One who gazes at fluffy clouds and
Notes they make shapes of kittens and strawberries.
I would only talk about Johnny Depp's eyes,
Ask if my bum looks big in this,
Talk about chocolate and periods,
Reflexology, colonic irrigation and Madonna and
My plaits being pulled at school,
That new rabbit-shaped jelly vibrator and foreplay,
And hot-sweat chilli-laced curry recipes,
Police car chases, violent vomit, Elvis and
Drunken tales of my next door neighbour
Accidentally breaking into my house when I was sleeping.

Salena Saliva Godden

York Hall, Bethnal Green *

See me there, I am waiting
I am waiting for first blood
See me, I am there
York Hall, Bethnal Green
In a Chinese bruise-blue split dress
The kind of girl you'd split a swollen eye over
I am waiting for pummelling muscle to pound sinew
Butcher tenderising and tearing meat tissue
For sweat to slip across the jabbing fist's hook
And cut thrust and rupture the Vaseline-greased eyebrow
Then the sound and the fury of the first sight of first blood
The bright stain is potent, vivid and sudden
Oily red, it drips, streams to the jaw-line
Racing breath and too fast an exhilarated heart beats
Water swilled into gaping mouths of plastic gum shield
Then spit bloodied spat in the bucket
The soaked-in salmon tint of the referees shirt
For the screaming girlfriend and the wife spilling her gin
For the mother's swinging handbag
For the huge bald oaf, the details of bulging brain
Thudding under his shiny pink, flabby skull skin
Feet of clay stupid and not boxing clever
See me there, I am waiting
For Spencer Wilding's keen and glorious triumph
His proud brother hollers, *Pure poetry in motion*
As his belaboured slack opponent falls to his knees in mercy
His arms cross his barrel-chest as he hits the stained canvas
Only fifty seconds into the second round   »

And the thrill of the slap of the count
For our hero raises his brawny arm victorious
And I never saw the champion boxer
Apologise modestly as he entered the ring or
Fight with one arm behind his back
And so, then to write that which would make one feel
Like first blood drawn, potent, vivid and sudden
Writing that is punched hard across the knuckles
And uppercut into a yellow plastic glove
No sullied apology or fey modesty
No holds barred and no clean fight
Ruddy welts pock and mark my bare-back against the ropes
Shadow boxing with a fist full of pages
I take off the gloves, bare-knuckled and as naked as
The sound and the fury of first blood
I am writing as if for first emphatic flood
See me here, I am waiting
I am waiting for first blood.

* *York Hall is a famous boxing venue in Bethnal Green, East London*

Alexander D Great
Grades of Grey *

Grey is the colour of the old man's hair
In the morning, when he rise,
Grey is the colour of the old man's chin
In the evening but his eyes
Are deep,
A deeper shade of black than the shadows cast
At the end of a grey day so overcast,
With a cloudy pint, in a bar,
Half asleep,
The old man sips and sighs.

> *Grades of grey, shades of grey*
> *Nothing black or white in the world of today*
> *Grades of grey with a grey overlay*
> *Grades of grades of grey.*

Grey is the colour of the Whitehall way
With the horseguards on parade,
Grey is the colour of the buildings bought
With money that was made
Long ago,
In a time when a man had no right to a name,
Like the red and black soldiers, pawns in the game,
Creamily gleaming Westminster
Aglow,
Grey of the highest grade...

> *Grades of grey, shades of grey*
> *Nothing black or white in the world of today*
> *Grades of grey with a grey overlay*
> *Grades of grades of grey.*

»

Grey is the colour of great Thamesis
On its journey to the sea.
White is the colour of the wake of the boats
Riding so easily
'pon the tide,
On the bank built of Blood Sugar bricks stands the Tate
Britannia in marble sits guarding the gate,
Cross over the bridge, dirty, mottled
And wide
To see a smoking chimney…

> *Grades of grey, shades of grey*
> *Nothing black or white in the world of today*
> *Grades of grey with a grey overlay*
> *Grades of grades of grey.*

Grey is the colour of the baby's eyes
In the push-chair by the door,
Black is the colour of his mother's lungs
As she looks at each store
Going by,
At the pink almshouses on the Wandsworth Road
Red/yellow McDonalds, grinning like a toad
At the BAC cream and brown
Try to fly
Then it's grey on grey as before...

> *Grades of grey, shades of grey*
> *Nothing black or white in the world of today*
> *Grades of grey with a grey overlay*
> *Grades of grades of grey.*

* Grades of Grey was commissioned as part of the Bus Jam performance project (2000), in which Apples & Snakes asked six artists to write a series of collaborative pieces which were performed unannounced on London buses.

Emma Hammond

babycake
my funny yellow fellow
slanty eyes astray
as you walk through the ashtray
with special fingers

would you not say

burning creating fiddling
stroking
my heart in a mouthful of chicky pie

apocryphal desire
i will miss your beanstalkliness
effortlessness
when you came around and round

walking down milsom st
in the raining rain
ran
past incense and mobiles
the crippled flautist
we smiled
at the pretty girls
oh you girl pink friend

together we meander
two dead bodies floating downstream
and you never yap yap yap

you always conquer

Choman Hardi
My Mother's Kitchen

I will inherit my mother's kitchen,
her glasses, some tall and lean, others short and fat,
her plates, an ugly collection from various sets,
cups bought in a rush on different occasions,
rusty pots she can't bear throwing away.
"Don't buy anything just yet," she says.
"Soon all of this will be yours."

My mother is planning another escape.
For the first time home is her destination,
the rebuilt house which she will furnish.
At 69 she is excited about starting from scratch.
It is her ninth time.

She never talks about her lost furniture
when she kept leaving her homes behind.
She never feels regret for things,
only her vine in the front garden
which spread over the trellis on the porch.
She used to sing for the grapes to ripen,
sew cotton bags to protect them from the bees.
But I know
I will never inherit my mother's trees.

Choman Hardi

What I Want

My father never had what he wanted
and we still don't have what he taught us to love.
For many years, he told us off
if he became aware of our loud earrings,
if we dressed in red or perfumed our hair.

He spoke of the neighbours
who were mourning the death of their sons,
of the poisoned and soulless villages,
of the Spring of '88, which was full of death.
He spoke of the end of the bigger war,
which meant further energy for destroying us.

Father cried
when he smelt the first daffodils of each spring,
when he saw images of the happy children
who weren't aware of what was happening.

In his despair he kept saying:
Like the American Indians,
our struggle will become a topic for films.

And I imagine what it would be like
to have what my father struggled for
and I imagine the neighbours
not visiting the graveyard in despair.

I imagine humane soldiers,
soldiers who would never say:
"We will take you to a place
where you will eat your own flesh."
And I imagine what it would be like
to have what my father struggled for.

Choman Hardi

Saqiz *

The women looked as if they were mourning;
scarves, Manto, trousers, shoes
and even socks were black and brown.
But when they got home,
they changed into their bright Kurdish outfits,
showed off their cleavages,
enhanced their curves
and put on their loose, see-through scarves.

What I miss is the calmness of summer evenings,
the slow pace of life, chatting on the grass,
eating melon, drinking icy water.
And the park that people escaped to,
where the young men found their future wives –
girls wrapped up like presents, waiting,
showing off a few strands of hair.

A Kurdish town in Iran where the author lived for 3 years

Karen Hayley

The Late Young Rowan Joffe

Who's infinitely hard to crack and tastes as sweet as toffee?
I'm talking about you my friend, the late young Rowan Joffe
Prop him up, invite him round, invite him in for coffee
The ubiquitous
Iniquitous
Spirituous Rowan Joffe

He'll move in like the Milk Tray man and swamp you with his style
And all because the lady hasn't eaten for a while

He'll hang upon your every word and make you a believer
And all because the lady loves a cronic self-deceiver

Yes, prop him up, soup him up, invite him in for coffee
The thought-provoking
Marlboro-smoking
Joking Rowan Joffe

Who's infinitely hard to crack and tastes as sweet as toffee?
Yes, I'm afraid it's you, my friend, the late young Rowan Joffe

Who's coveted and criticised, idolised and cursed?
Who's got his prep school hang-ups and an English double first?
Invite him in your hearts, ladies, and let him do his worst

That muscle man
That Peter Pan
The lonely Rowan Joffe

The real McCoy
The boy
The one and only Rowan Joffe

John Hegley

Poet with bag

John Hegley

No to tiddlywinks

John Hegley

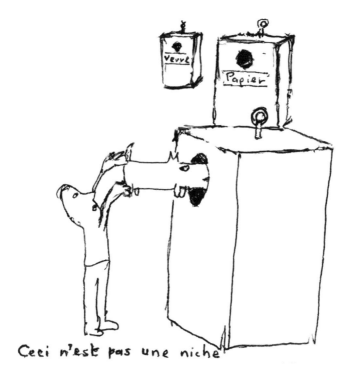

Ceci n'est pas une niche

John Hegley

Hilaire

La mère, La mer

You write to me your recurring dream:
of approaching the sea,
drawn to its vastness,
your anticipation of plunging in its salty breadth,
to dive through the breakers,
to be buoyed on your back,
arms stretched,
embracing the sky,
slowly tossed and buffeted
like a cork
and then gathering your body together
unfolding again
down through the water
which touches every bit of you
softly
more than your husband ever has
(this last, conjecture);
but always
some slight mishap,
a towel or bathers forgotten,
prevents your immersion.
This is not a dream I would share,
frightened of its symbolism,
but you write it to me
and seem unaware of what you reveal:
your life's metaphor
your silenced sexuality
your inability to swim.

Hilaire

manifest

he walks towards me through the bar
pint in one hand
glass of red in the other.
nicely balanced.
clocks me,
locks his gaze on mine.
it's in his hips
the not quite swagger
the cocksure stride.
it's on his lips
the grin about to break
and in between
the flicker of his tongue
a quirk to help him concentrate
on spilling none.
deep within his eyes
lies certainty
this is the one.

this is the one.

Kazuko Hohki
Looking for Me

I've been looking for somebody
Who represents exactly me.
No confusion, no misunderstanding
With us, love will be so easy

Looking for me,
Looking for me
That's what you do to love
Looking for me
Looking for me
To be happy eternally

I've been missing the information
Sent from the institute of love
How to find my replica, my clone
Where's the creator gone?

Looking for me,
Looking for me
That's what you do to love
Looking for me
Looking for me
We'll be happy eternally

»

You say love needs mystery,
Can't survive without mystery
I am always a mystery
Don't think I'm big-headed.

Looking for me,
Looking for me
That's what you do to love
Looking for me
Looking for me
We'll be happy internally

This is the finale song from my multimedia solo show called My Husband Is a Spaceman. I performed a work-in-progress version of this show at Apples & Snakes event at BAC café in 1999. That time the show was not very multimedia except I had a chair. In 2000, I sang this song at the Apples & Snakes website launch party, again at BAC cafe. That time the show was slightly more multimedia and I had my animation on a video with a backing track and I even had David Woods from Ridiculusmus doing a backing chorus singing, ooo la la la, ooo la la la. The event was packed and I remember asking the audience to light up their lighters in the end of the song (there are two choruses and lighting up lighters feels very natural) and some people did. Apples & Snakes collect nice smokers.

Michael Horovitz

Some Poets Are Politicians...

Poets are the unacknowledged legislators of the world
– PB Shelley, A Defence of Poetry

Some poets are politicians,
    some are truth-hounds, some electricians.
Andrew Motion's butler voice, elocuted diction
    smoothing out every crinkle of latent friction
    comes on stern and upstanding across the air,
    Saint Sincere
    ventriloquising Tony Blair
    (though mercifully
    digging a heel in
    against our People's
    PM's fatal flaw,
    that vainglorious lust
    for power through war).
Niggle-mouthed Northern bloke of the folk
    Sean O'Brien throws testy punches as fraught
    as yer pit bull terrier John Prescott, caught
    between a protester, two Jags,
    his official line and his lunch.
Don Paterson's Charles Kennedy with a skinful of nag.
Tom Paulin on telly's Ann Widdecombe in drag.

But not all living bards are chess-move politicians.
Wendy Cope's Glenda Jackson. C A Duffy's Clare Short.
Geoffrey Hill's a broody Gwyneth Dunwoody.
Pinter bleeds for peace in a righteous moody.
Kathleen Raine's milk of paradise   »

could still feed our needs.
Seamus Heaney's Richard Taylor – wise, concise
neighbourhood physician.

Tony Harrison's Tony Benn,
a mouthful-of-nails electrician
as nifty dispensing home truths in bulk
as debunking Dome myths of that ilk
spun by Mandy Pandy
and those wiggling worms of the silk,
fatboots Charlie, merry Derry
and Cherie-laced counsel
for the President,
Kubla Tone.

Johns Hegley and Agard, R McGough and Grace Nichols
twitch that trustworthy touchstone,
the serious funnybone
of real life that tickles
hard songlines into action.
Let's give thanks for such poets
who give satisfaction
with the bonus of laughter
Stevie Smith and Betjeman quested after,
and with no Party Card or flag
save the insights and truths
of inspiration unfurled
to arm them for a deeper
legislation of the world.

Mahmood Jamal

Love Poem

Rusty joints hold hard
Movement must be bold
towards the dust if love
would grow and flower
before it dies.

That strings in garlands
broke in hands, the flowers
which were ours withered
we could not endure.

We were caught flying
brought low by clouds
that misted all our dreams
and tears, splintered broke
to soak our burning love.

That trees turn leafless
life briefly withers snows
turns cold, slowed us down.
We drown in uncertainty
to show us where to go!

As we sit cold and wet
with old remembrance we
glance upwards thinking
from sick hearts what hope
might start, break loose
before we die.   »

Perhaps today the clouds part,
here the rainbow ends
summer begins and mends
our broken hearts
and we leap together to fly.

Mark Gwynne Jones
Cuckoo in a Clock

"I don't know where the day's
gone," she sighed;
as if surprised not to find it in the drugs
cabinet. Or having a bath, perhaps,
with the water

hot. But of course
it never was. The day had indeed
gone. In boxes carried by the dustbin men
out towards the edge
of town, ready

to be buried with yesterday's.
It disappeared, like that golden orb,
over the urban horizon. Taking with it
the birdsong she never heard,
the sunlit brook

she never saw and a cool
breeze. Fleet of foot and swift of soul
it passed this way an hour ago.
It tiptoed round you whilst you read
and turning to the door

left. Burning up
    a flight of stairs
three streets and an afternoon
before you even knew. Funny, because,
when you did know   »

and watched it through
the office window,
it sat on its hands and pretended to be going...
nowhere, but,
cuckoo in a clock.

Mark Gwynne Jones

Little Lamb

Little lamb, who made thee?
Dost thou know who made thee?
Gave thee life and bid thee feed
On blood and guts of old dead sheep:
Gave thee clothing of delight,
A ton of wool you drag behind:
Gave thee such a tender voice
bleating in the slaughterhouse:
Little lamb who made thee,
Dost thou know who made thee?

Little lamb, I'll tell thee,
It was Dr Wilmut of the Roslin Institute.
Who in a bid to help him sleep
Cloned you from another sheep.
Believing that the counting game
Would work if each one was the same…
Little lamb, God bless thee
Little lamb, God bless thee...

Jackie Kay
Childhood, Still

The sun is out and so is childhood – remember
How the summer droned its song forever.

Three small girls tumble down the steep hill.
Grass skips, gust makes their skirts frill.

A wee boy scoots towards the big blue loch.
His fishing net bigger than his baw face.

It's hot; there's a breeze like a small caught breath.
This is it; these are the days that never stop.

Childhood ticks, tocks, ticks. Metronome.
Speaking clock. Sand glass. Time bomb.

A boy kicks a ball through a window, smashes
A gaping hole, but this is childhood still

Where big things grow small: small as a petal
Or a freckle on a face, a speckle

On an egg, or as small as a tadpole,
Small as the space where the ball missed the goal,

As dot to dot, as a crumb of Mrs Jack's cake,
Small as the silver locket around her neck.

The long grass whines in the high wind.
Away in the distance, the church bells chime.

Childhood ticks, tocks, ticks. Metronome.
Speaking clock. Sand glass. Time bomb.

Suddenly: the clatter of boots in the street.
The sob of a white van speeding away.   »

The cries of a small boy alone in a stairwell.
This is childhood; this is childhood as well.

The policeman caught by the Candyman.
A town's sleep murdered by the Sandman.

There goes the janitor, the teacher, the priest,
Clergyworker, childminder, careworker. *Wheesht.*

The auntie, the uncle, the father, the mother;
Opening and closing and opening the door.

Childhood ticks, tocks, ticks. Metronome.
Speaking clock. Sand glass. Time bomb.

Oh There she goes.
Oh There she goes.
Peerie heels and pointed toes.
Look at her feet. She thinks she's neat.
Black stockings and dirty feet.

Remember the toadstool, the promise of a chrysalis,
The taste of lemon bon bons, the taste of liquorice.

The past keeps calling the children back.
Number six: pickup sticks. Tick tack, Tick tack.

The clock hands crawl, August's slow talk.
Autumn comes: the snap and crackle of amber leaves.

There's a brand new friend waiting in the school,
A gleam in her eye, ready for Tig or marbles or skipping.

Skip, skop to the barber's shop, Keepie-Uppie, Kerbie.
Bee Baw Babbity, Following Wee Jeannie.

Green peas and Barley. Okey Kokey. My mummy told me.
Stotty. Peever. Thread the needle. The Big Ship sails.

This is childhood, oh let it be childhood still.

Fatimah Kelleher

Perfect Madness

In one moment of perfect madness
I've scaled heights this feeble body
Could never hope to reach
Stroked the scarred chest of a sadness
My hopes and fears have often preached
Answered questions that my whole life
I have failed to even seek

Elusive as purity
I've held hands with Absolute Surety
In dungeons offering a thousand doors
I've Travelled floors covered with a million tiles
Each gently whispering countless thoughts
With artless guile

Devoid of all sanity
I joined Kingship to Anarchy
With matrimonial ribbons and seals
Brokered deals between right and wrong
In conflicts where warriors terrorised battlefields
With tears and love songs

In one moment of perfect madness
I've grasped the logic of chaos
Through the window of a hangman's noose
Abstained from passion and pleasure
Whilst sipping on the finest apple juice
In that one perfectly tuned moment,
I knew illusion to be the only Truth

Mimi Khalvati

Pantoum after Gauguin

How do you see this tree? Is it really green?
Use green then, the most beautiful green on your palette.
And the gold of their bodies? Living gold you mean?
Make love to that gold and make it a habit.

Use green then, the most beautiful green on your palette,
to shadow the world always chained to your feet.
Make love to that gold and make it a habit
to leave love eternally incomplete.

To shadow the world always chained to your feet,
don't be afraid of your most brilliant blues.
To leave love eternally incomplete,
nothing shines more than the love you will lose.

Don't be afraid of your most brilliant blues
for night phosphorescences bloom like flowers.
Nothing shines more than the love you will lose,
these are lovers' bouquets with miraculous powers.

For night phosphorescences bloom like flowers
on the innocent ground where your memories lie.
These are lovers' bouquets with miraculous powers
where all the colours of the spectrum die.

On the innocent ground where your memories lie,
how will you paint what memory sees?
Where all the colours of the spectrum die,
memory's blind to flowers and trees.   »

How will you paint what memory sees?
And the gold of their bodies? Living gold you mean?
Memory's blind to flowers and trees.
How do you see this tree? Is it really green?

Shamshad Khan

I've been waiting for funding so long *

my performance idea
for a motorised-mini skirt
with automatic cold weather reflex
has had time to go out of fashion
and
come back in again.

the funding criteria seemed clear:
vision and imagination, quality of execution,
creativity of approach, capacity to
encourage public involvement in art.

my application failed

I tried again

they just
loved the new proposal:
razzle dazzle tunic with pinstripe shalvaar
and union jack head scarf

cross cultural couture
positive action
sure to get a reaction
new audiences
targeted and marketed.

next step, the media.
very keen.   »

"the programming's no problem.
we've got the ideal slot

asian relationships and arranged marriages"

they like a hook
and usually find one size fits all.

I decide to risk it. Any publicity is
publicity.
we're on air.

"could you say a little about –
how you see the pinstripe *shall waar* as a symbolic representation of
post colonial South Asia. a floating signifier
rupturing cross cultural re-appropriation
of your cultural heritage"

I'm thinking about admitting
I was just taking the piss. but she's taken my pause
to conclude I'm not so quick.

she's already re-phrasing
"can I put it this way

if you were forced into an arranged marriage
would you be able to wear an outfit
like the one you've created
or would this be totally unacceptable to your community"

* *Any similarity to funding bodies or institutions is entirely intentional. The writer would like to thank NWAB for their continued support of her work.*

Shamshad Khan

love – over-eating and over-hearing

you listen to music in the same way you eat food
with reverent ecstasy

tasting each cadence in sound
separating layers of rhythm
savouring slithers of melting melody
whilst hearing salt grind
in the unexpected sweet refrain
held at the back of your throat
the deepest base
touches the tip of your tongue
so sourness sings
its sharp twist
to curdle drums

you peel a piano concentrating on keeping the spiral
flavour spins the radio dial
blur of colliding in your headphones

in the wet street a woman and a man argue about
who should have rung who

on rainy days I'm told
everything tastes like music.

Mike Ladd

Taking Back the Airplane (a hyphenated ghazal)

We lay on our rooftop, our hearts like the sky
The children are sleeping, dreaming in sky

Fourth Avenue stretches as far as the sea
Streetlights mute starlight and dampen the sky

We stretch like snow angels, gazing where stars
Are replaced by airplanes landing through sky

In the line of their flight pattern, we witness the light
Glimmer like lemur eyes off in the sky

Tiny at first, afraid of the earth
Beams hover in night and order the sky

Like watching your frame in a rainforest mist
The airplanes fly into their shape in the sky

My thumbs in your palm, sifting our history
I squeeze on your veins when planes break the sky

When a jet is above, you gather my hands
The rumble is distant, you feel like the sky

Traffic and blood vessels move the same way
I have seen it in movies obsessed with sky

I wake in our towel, your side my horizon
I have dreamt of our families shipped through this sky

Mike Ladd

Let's Discuss Disgusting (after George Clinton)

To Charles Murray, author of the Bell Curve, *which tried to prove most folks of color were genetically inferior to whites. To white artists who think using the word 'nigger' in the 90s is daring and controversial (Best read in a British accent)*

Ick-a-brick-a-my-brain
I'm-a-sick-a-cracker-shit
Ick-a-brick-a-my-brain
I'm-a-sick-a-cracker-shit
Ick-a-brick-on-my-brain
I'm-a-sick-of-cracker-shit

Their game is to drive me insane
with insult on insult
thrown like dirt
but dirt don't hurt 'less God's out of work
which she probably is in this jive-ass economy
no harmony mentally
if I can't make a dollar
they gonna holler somethin' wrong with me
plenty be through with the Catch 22
so some sling rock, others bend to get screwed
but most of us is standing 'gainst the wind like we been doin'
impatient with the nation tryin to keep the circulation movin'
cuz we don't freeze up and fall asleep
it's time to kill three kings and feed Jesus to the sheep
cuz Sony bought the rights to his cross last week

The Vatican is renting out the shroud to David Letterman
he bought for it for Madonna
But Iacocca's in the bed again   »

Cracker lady drove her cracker babies to the river Hades
shit is sick and crazy like
Mike and Bobby Brady
swapping bloody undies with
Ed, Gene and Ted Bundy
If genetics cause connections, it's
Mass murder and the pecks
if they can't figure how we breathe
they simply break our necks

Ick-a-brick-a-my-brain
I'm-a-sick-a-cracker-shit
Ick-a-brick-on-my-brain
I'm-a-sick-a-cracker-shit
Ick-a-brick-on-my-brain
I'm-a-sick-a-cracker-shit

Once again I awoke with a gun in my mouth
Made to Rape in the USA
engraved on the silver side
each bullet brought to you by the mental side of genocide
I thought it was the cops
with the barrel to my head...
It was the Doo-Doo-Crack-
Honky-Dory-Burn-in-Ball-a-Glory-heads
of quasi-intellectuals
perpetual brain killers working off of fear
ready to kill us all, Bitches, Niggas, Spicks and Queers
See they got to make it feasible appease-able to white liberals
Forget hypothetically
genetically we criminals

Little peckerwood party pooper press heads
Rex Von-Shmitt Harvard graduates
gonna resurrect some biological experiments
masturbation by phrenology   »

perverted gynecology of the brain
if the IQ gives clues, it's to who's insane

Ick-a-brick-on-my-brain
I'm-a-sick-of-cracker-shit
Ick-a-brick-a-my-brain
I'm-a-sick-a-cracker-shit
Ick-a-brick-a-my-brain
I'm-a-sick-a-cracker-shit

Let's discuss disgusting

The Bell Curve, death by statistics and verbs
and adjectives such as
"stupid Kaffir herb"
a book full of tobacco spit
regurgitated cracker shit
stuck a lynch mob in a tux, wiped its ass and simply packaged it
One deep South cow patty
with a ribbon on it
New Republic gumming on the edge
like the shit was Blue Bonnet
Got to bring it up as a legitimate question
"should we kill the niggers now or should we teach 'em a lesson?"
Muthafuckin' periodical systematic with methodical
disempowerment disembowelment of the brown
it's so easy to win a race when the competition's beat down

But we never been really beat
with one soul, we rule the streets
son's got a gun and granny got chicken feet

Chuck Murray vision blurry
from mental masturbation in the girlie magazines of the far right
text books of death   »

sayin' "fuck what you heard, Holocaust is just a word for
bad breath"
But halitosis kings up a toast to racism
cuz that makes cash fast and scapegoating helps the system

Ick-a-brick-a-my-brain
I'm-a-sick-a-cracker-shit
Ick-a-brick-a-my-brain
I'm-a-sick-a-cracker-shit
Ick-a-brick-on-my-brain
I'm-a-sick-a-cracker-shit

Let's discuss disgusting

Now, how are we supposed to be genetically inferior?
they're scaring ya with all this cracker guy hysteria
just cuz we survive in Africa while whitey gets malaria…
but serious, I'm delirious with this question
folks of color studied their identity since the first suggestion
of the other
and now they scream PC threatens whitey and his lovers
all we did is ask the cracker man to try and understand himself
But he couldn't so he wrote book and blamed shit on someone else
again!
we better count our friends
cuz the battle's been going and it's gettin to the end
Cracker dude, ain't you sick-a all this cracker shit too?
and all the cracker blues they been puttin' on you
Cracker woman, ain't your cracker bosom sick-a swellin' up with lies?
And all this cracker jargon trying to claim between your thighs?
don't forget the cracker niggas who can't figure out the problem,
but still will grill the president
and are sick of crackers robbing our livelihood
                              neighborhood
                              human good   »

Peckerwoods
packaging your children's breath
and selling it to Hollywood
We are genetically superior Mr Quentin Tarentino
humans are baaaad Muthafuckas
from Flatbush to Reo
I'll stuff Newt Gingrich's nose into Sterno
turn his brains into porridge
and ask him one question...

Does the sign on my lawn say *Dead Cracker Storage*?!
Does the sign on my lawn say *Dead Cracker Storage*!?
Does the sign on my lawn say *Dead Cracker Storage*!

Ick-a-brick-a-sick-a-spick-a
Sick-a-crack-a
Sick-a-nigg-a
Sick-a-dyke-a
Sick-a-kike-a

I guess it's time we get a new lawn

Mike Ladd
The Survival of Vinyl

Once I traded five pounds
of Sydney Bichet
for twelve pounds of funk
the deal wasn't done on weight
it's how I've come to know
these galaxies on vinyl
four thousand line my walls
a feeble attempt at mastering
a universe

Instead I'm overwhelmed
the load fits in fifteen boxes
each at fifty pounds
from Northampton to New York
to Boston
the bulk, a stone pinball
pushed by me as Sisyphus

No one will master this universe
the jackets wear in circles
succumbing to the disk
as mysterious
as Os in crops

Coltrane's got a crease but
place him on the plate
and you will spin with rings
each pop a moon
a skip is a slip in dimensions
and the sounds   »

the sounds? – Man's latest
discovery is that the brain
is so big they know
nothing of it so,
go figure

Go figure
Interstellar Space
I rather let it slide from
the jacket
teach the needle
and leave me weightless
with more mass
than a pin
from a Sun

Ra could ford
milky ways of tones
better than I swallow
stars of notes
so many in a groove
I choose the grind of
Maggot Brain
to rumble through my chord

When I was eight
I owned headphones
my trowel
for my mother's stacks
A giant chair faced
knobs and crates
there I found the *Axis*
Bold as Love
a bus built with steel strings
rolled hard from one ear

»

through my head
to the other
I tried to follow it
with the backs of my eyes
this is the bus I ride as passenger
on what I tried to own
these stacks go on forever

The Bichet was my father's
an unaccounted inheritance
which I lost like his dog tags
for a nuzzle after gym
He was an archeologist
with a million shards of
pots all in a room
hoarded like records
in an attempt to make
sense of something
as basic as utensils
the space between notes
the gaps in electrodes
or the funk between stars

Inge Elsa Laird
fragments

like fragments
  it ends
I stare on, hide in my shelter
watch the old man
carry her mutilated body
I look into her frozen eyes
remember the afternoon
when we played with our miniature
  teaset

  one cup, one saucer
  a teapot, a jug

all afternoon we played

"will you stay?" "No," says my mother

black fragments the memory
  one cup, one saucer

Inge Elsa Laird

Time is time again
denounce sorrow, grief
walk on – then
no longer awaiting
but exploring
    enacting
the pace – the inner room
    of love

now pause and listen
    to the whisper
the gentle chatter
    of light and sound
    of light and sound

Inge Elsa Laird
allegria / autumn leaves

tone tonality of colours
sweep past with rhythms
that speak of innovation

in conversation water
ripples over stone beds
sea trout leap into
light and air
music takes wing

Fran Landesman
Black and White

Sitting with my friend Stella
In a parked car, on a hot summer day,
In the segregated city of St Louis
With the great Oscar Peterson
And his bass player Al McKibben.
Two white girls and two black musicians.

Across the street, staring our way
Three big, sweaty, white men.
We stayed schtum,
When they crossed the street as one.
Leaning hairy arms
On the windows of our car,
They peered inside.
Then one of them cleared his throat.
"Mr Peterson," he said,
"Could I have your autograph?"

Liz Lochhead

My Way

I only did it for a laugh
I did it because I'm a fool for love
I did it because push had come to shove
I did it because – my age – I've got nothing to prove

But I did it
I did it
I did it
Yes I did

I did it to settle an argument with a friend
I did it to drive our Hazel round the bend
I did it to get one over on our kid
I did it to nip it in the bud
I did it that way because I couldn't stand the sight of blood

But I did it
I did it
I did it
Yes I did

I did it to bury the hatchet and get a night's sleep
I did it to get out before I was in too deep
I did it to piss on his chips and put his gas at a peep

But I did it
I did it
I did it
Mea absolutely culpa, me!   »

I did it to go out in a blaze of glory
I did it to make them listen to my side of the story
I only did it to get attention
I did it to get an honourable mention
I did it to put an end to it all
I did it for no reason at all

But I did it
I did it
I did it
Yes I did

Jared Louche
the tiniest heart

the tiniest heart I've ever seen,
the gentlest beats I've ever felt,
fluttering delicate as silkworm's weave,
hope filling as saffron winds
bluster and breathe.

clutched in my hands a gentle thing,
dropped from my hands a broken thing.

I took all this from you.
I took all this from me.

I turned my head and caught a glimpse
a sidelong glance of passion pure,
no barb, no hook, no borderline
a touch so light that smoothed my mind
and brushed my hair.

I turned my head and caught a snare,
a jagged snare that tore a hole,
a ragged hole the shape of fright
a fright which left me without sight.

I took all this from you.
I took all this from me.

it felt like sailing in those arms,
like swaying, sweeping, singing seas
that washed my back and bent my knees,

»

a haven safer than the place
that grew my sapling heart
from seed, now flowered to tree.

sparks jumped shocks from my flint fists
and burned through summer's sweet love nests
then poured black ash into my chest.

I took all this from you.
I took all this from me.

Paul Lyalls

Any Bus Stop in England

He was one
They were more
He is gone
They are above the law
He was a son
He was young
His life had just begun
But just like the bus
That didn't come
His journey was over
Before it'd really begun.

They walk
He is still
They talk
His thoughts chill
Denied even a single thought
While those that kill
Roam free at will
Living goes on
In a world of different skin
His life brightly shone
Remembered as a beautiful thing
Change takes so long
But change we have to bring
Until the hatred is gone
And like the bus that doesn't come
Next time it may be your son.

Stacy Makishi

Between

Between.
Between 6 and
7 o'clock.
I always hated this time of day, especially on Sundays.
I could never understand why I was called in from my weekend's
mud pies and marble games,
to watch Walter Cronkite on the news.
It was like watching laundry tumble dry.
Walter Cronkite's mouth is a giant tumble drier
and the troubles of the world tumble, tumble and tumble,
but never dry.

I met her on a bus while lost in Kalihi.
Nothing seemed familiar.
She was wearing a calico flowered dress.
No. She wasn't.
Calico was on my mind, not on her.
I don't remember what she was wearing.
Only that her hands reminded me of my Grandpa,
the way his hands were calmly clasped as they laid him to rest.
"Heaven or hell, Grandpa?," I once asked.

"Purgatory, girl. Das' da way I like it. Right in between."
His clasped hands formed a small rib cage holding a heart.

Between 6 and 7 o'clock one Sunday,
I had to use the toilet real bad.
My brother was in the bathroom
(for what seemed to be the weekend)   »

Walter Cronkite was tumbling in the living room,
and I knew I had to use the restaurant's toilet outside.
We lived near three restaurants.
Hawaiian foods, Korean foods and Italian foods owned
by the Vietnamese.
They all shared one toilet, which ran between our apartments.
These toilets were used only during emergencies.
Big emergencies.
This was a big emergency.

I had, however, a rather paranoid relationship with that toilet,
more specifically, with that toilets' window.
As a child, I spent many hours peeking through that window.
I liked to watch unsuspecting toilet-users strip down
to their most vulnerable forms
to perform the most human of tasks.
But I didn't watch them out of judgment,
but rather out of humility, for I knew no greater act of honesty.
And as karmic retribution goes,
what comes around, goes around.
I could never go around there with much ease,
squatting over that toilet
my eyes were fixed upon that window
awaiting judgment.
Did I feel guilt or shame there?
I guess guilt requires a conscience.
Shame requires an audience.

Sunday.
I can't remember if it was her name,
or the name of the day.
I don't know what made her take my hand.
Maybe she sensed my fear of being lost.
We got off at the next stop.   »

I never let go of her hand.
We talked a lot.
Mostly we talked about nothing.
Mostly we talked with our hands:

a squeeze, a brush, a stroke,

between.

Between is always the most intense place for me.
Notice how you breathe differently when you're in between.
When a hand
slowly dips into your pants...
into your panties,
the brief
second before it's
in between
your

legs.

That's the place that I call *the between*,
where your breath is
short
and
few
in between.

Or between can be
between 6 and 7 o'clock on Sunday.
The impending doom of Monday morning but you're not there
to deal with it yet,
no, you're in between the joys of the weekend.
Between heaven and hell
to contemplate, to dread, to tumble.   »

With her hand she motions, this is my house.
I stand on one step and I'm now as tall as she.
My heart contracts as I dangle.
I am drawing in close now as a moon.
I am her satellite.
She is my world revolving.
I smell baby's breath.
I see calico flowers.

Two lips part.
I tumble guilt. I tumble shame

between her lips.

I am in a bathroom
staring up at a window.
It is between 6 and 7 o'clock on Sunday
and I am in between.

Nicholas 'Urbanspirit' Makoha

Psalm

I have been to heaven and back twice
Seen God comb the stars to peer through your eyes
Wrestled with the Devil to possess your caress
To perform your love as mine

I have tamed the sun from its burn
Taught wisdom to recognise who you are
Infected dreams with your memory
And drawn your heart in the storm

I have anointed my spirit with your name
Nurtured my joy to soak your pain
Neglected my joy for your foolishness
Washed my transgressions in the pool of your divine mind

I have spoken my love for you in tongues
Hidden secrets in prophets' arms
Instructed your oppression to claim my freedom as thine
To perform your love as mine

Nicholas 'Urbanspirit' Makoha

Who Do They Say That I Am?

They say that I am
Three words short of a proverb
Two beliefs shy of a religion
One god less to believe in

They say that I am
Three tribes short of a people
One heart less of than couple
Two breaths closer to death

They say that I am
Three friends this side of Judas
Two betrayals shy of Brutus
One wisdom short of Confucius

They say that I am
Three sins past temptation
Two generations behind emancipation
One prayer beyond frustration

They say that I am
Three tears short of a river
Two waters deep of leaders
One hope less than a believer

They say that I am
Three nomads shy of a footprint
Two lullabies from a lament
One witness short of a testament

They say that I am
Three chains left of a slave
Two victories short of the brave
One coffin to the right of the grave

Nicholas 'Urbanspirit' Makoha

Sinai

If I lose you at the water
I will find you at the mountain
You know how I thirst
But I've got to get there first

There is a river where waters are daylight
A soul whose springs are nightshade
And a land where the two waters meet
Joy as my love bathes in these pools

She introduced herself as all my next breaths
Her dreams auditioned to become my realities
Forcing me to exhale all my sufferings
I tried to survive in the perfumes of my yesterdays
But found she had stitched her name in the collar of my soul

Yet every time I showed her my love
She hid in her wounds
And camouflaged her tears
That watered the garden of her days

Her deepest memories began to assume
That I too was groomed
In the armour of her past loves
Who had scarred her heart with swords of promises

And so I was crucified for such care
Still, in the silence that binds all moments together
I tried to, believe me I tried to
keep this echo inside myself
That is when the mountain moved

Aoife Mannix
Only the Essentials

I pack my suitcase with soda pop sunshine,
the bubbles of swinging afternoons,
an empty vodka bottle,
the pink ceramic pig I smashed open,
eating the pennies inside,
barely enough for the plane ticket.
A warped ashtray,
some cigarette papers on which to write my dreams,
a stack of curling postcards,
a silver alligator with a detachable tail,
I hold him up for luck,
letting his metal tears burn my skin,
chocolate scars, spinning bottle kisses,
a kidnapping shouted from a window,
throwing my knickers in the street,
gate crashing through love,
and passing out on the bathroom floor.
Mickey Mouse, Donald Duck, my battered teddy bear,
the drawings my brother gives me of miniature supermen,
his faith in the Incredible Hulk, and other spiritual talismans,
my mother's instructions to eat properly,
a set of playing cards, all those gin rummy nights,
the jack of spades a handsome devil.
I crush in a few more prayers, the feathers I plan to wear,
my platform shoes to make me taller,
my grandmother's Celtic cross to make me stronger,
a silver bracelet with roaring lions' heads.   »

I fold my courage and wonder how to squeeze in my heart,
a tattered worn out jacket with patches on the sleeves,
the crazy man under my window singing in the moonlight,
the boy on the other side of the wall practicing his drums,
the hum of the fish tank, the endless cups of tea dunked in rhythm,
my only love song radio station,
and all the scattered pieces of my home
that suddenly seem so utterly, entirely essential.

Aoife Mannix

From the Wreckage ✣

I have survived
the closing of doors,
your voice slurred on the answering machine,
walking barefoot over an ocean of glass,
kissing your cheek in the crematorium,
the endless shaking of hands,
the doling out of sandwiches,
the silences between cups of tea,
cigarettes smoked to the butt,
the ticking of boxes, rain on Sunday afternoons,
the missing of trains, waiting for something to happen,
rooms so small you can't breathe,
words I can't pronounce,
that time I nearly drowned,
long walks home when there were no taxis,
early mornings, waiting rooms, white coats, test results,
even the look on your face when you said goodbye.

> *Goodbye Piccadilly, farewell Leicester Square*
> *It's a long, long way to Tipperary but my heart lies there*

Tonight, it's still raining like it has been for days.
You think you're in a ship at sea,
the wind bashing the windows
waves against the side of the ferry.
You ask me again, "where am I?"
I'm tempted to imagine us someplace else,
but know you never had much patience for my idle dreaming. »

"We're in the hospice, Mammy."
To my surprise, you laugh.
"For a moment there, I thought we were in the piggy boat."
I'm not sure what this means,
but it sounds funny so I find myself laughing too.
I grab your hand,
after all, this is the last trip we'll ever take together.
It does feel as if we're rolling slowly across the Atlantic Ocean.
Instead of stuck in a small room with you in the bed and me
in the armchair.
As impersonal as a hotel.
The ghosts of other travelers disappearing round corners
before we can catch up with them to ask where they're going.

She died of the fever and no one could save her
And that was the end of Sweet Molly Malone

I wish I could save you from being washed away from us.
I can see you're getting weaker, but you never were one for giving in.
My mattress on the floor a floating raft,
I hold your hand as tight as I can, but it's four in the morning
and no one is coming to help us.
Your skin like a baby's, loose over the bone.
I watch fascinated that you're getting younger,
the years peeling away till you're light as paper.
We're traveling back in time together.
You close your eyes and begin without any introduction.
This is to be your final performance,
this is what you're leaving me with.
All those songs you used to sing now come back to haunt us,
like this is my very last chance to learn the words.
You do a lullaby and then a prayer. »

God bless Mammy, oh wasn't it fun in the bath tonight
With the hot so hot and the cold so cold, God bless Daddy I almost forgot

Then comes a nursery rhyme, and after that a hail of quotations,
snatches of tunes I've heard you sing a thousand times before,
now all strung together,
as your life flashes before my eyes.
Lady MacBeth washing her hands,
suddenly we can both see the dagger, and I beg you to stop.
You move on to your favourite prison in the wilderness,
and how love kills.

This is by far the longest night of my life.
This is deep in the eye of the storm,
this is you and me, outside of history,
breathing nothing but water.

Ride on, see you
I could never go with you, no matter how I wanted to
Ride on, see you
I could never go with you, no matter how I wanted to

* From the Wreckage was commissioned by Apples & Snakes as part of
Writers on the Storm (2002), a theatrical poetry production and tour.

Roger McGough
The Last Strike *

On Monday next
Undertakers are going on strike.
Crematorium workers and gravediggers
Will be coming out in deepest sympathy.

A state of emergency is to be declared.
Soldiers who can be spared
From driving fire-engines, trains and bread vans
Will be called in to bury the dead.

Throughout the country
There have been reports of widespread
Panic-dying.

I remember my night at the Roebuck Arms, January 22nd 1983. At the time I was still living in Liverpool and wanting to move to London, so my three days down there were spent looking at flats and houses around Notting Hill. In fact I moved to Portobello Road in the following July. I still have in my diary the running order of the poems I read that evening (as well as Mandy Williams' telephone number and details of my £100 fee). One poem I read that evening but was never published, although I will be including it in my forthcoming Collected Poems (Penguin) is this one.

Adrian Mitchell
to all our friends

August
blue seas for ever
a spicy breeze
bear us towards an ancient island

the harbour opens its arms to us
in an embrace
of boats with clinking masts
brown children leaping over ropes
donkeys fishermen dogs
women with baby bundles
shadow cats
and the sun
shining down upon a maze
of whitewashed alleys
leading up towards
bright domes and shining towers
and beyond all these
the dark hills of enchantment

we have come home
to the island which we've been creating
for so many years
with our buckets and spades

and here we all stand
with salt spray in our eyes
makers of dreamcakes and mudpies

Mr Social Control
Spoken Word

The spoken word is the original form of creativity.
When God created the world
He said, "Let there be light."
He didn't send an e-mail
called "re: Light", to formless@void
from god@everywhere.is

Patrick Neate
Chongololo (Centipede)

When we met at Mr Kapotwe's gallery
You commanded the space
You were standing with your head kinked to one side
Your neck long like a Makonde sculpture
Indian earrings
Hair wrapped
In a sunflower doek

From the start
It was a look
I mistook
For an interest
In art

I was staring at you nostalgically
As if you were already a memory
You, at the picture of the chongololo
In the warm colours
We see
Before a storm
Is upon us
And the first thing you said to me
Was
– The chongololo has so many legs
But it can never run
Off the canvas

I remember that   »

I have since seen so much art
In so many different contexts
With you standing
Next to me
The Brazilian Salgado's
Pictures of Africa
In a Delhi gallery –
Rachel Whiteread's
Castings of hidden spaces –
Makonde in mahogany
With your face
And neck.
Sectioned off
For acquisitive tourists
In a Maputo gift shop –
Or
Samuel Fosso
In a fashionable
Parisian studio
Best-dressed as Mobutu
Holding a yellow sunflower
As if all power
Was right there
In ubuntu –
And Edward Hopper
In the Met
I can't forget
That you were bored
Ignored
The pathos
Found in pictures of men
Staring out of windows.
Those same pictures that made
My chest heave   »

As, eternally,
Those knowing fools were condemned to watch their youth
Take its leave –

We crossed borders with glee
You and me
In and of and against the world
Drunk like
Global village idiots
Like this was as good
As it could ever get

And yet
Most of all I remember
The chongololo in Mr Kapotwe's gallery
I wonder if you knew then
Sometimes, somehow
I guess I even wonder if you planned this
That when the storm came
We wouldn't escape the frame
And, for all our legs,
Could never flee this ever-shrinking canvas

Grace Nichols
Catching Up on the Classics

from a sequence of poems about the Muse in London

No two ways she was slumming it,
she who'd only raised golden goblets
to her lips and felt
the proud blood of the gods
coursing through her spirits,

Now sits in the corner of an English pub
taking half-beer sips,
Ovid's *Metamorphosis* in one hand,
in the other a packet of crisps,
quietly catching up on the classics.

Whose fault is it if some bloke leers her down –
"Come on love, show us your tits."
Whose fault is it, if on leaving
she accidentally spills
the foamy dregs about him.

Whose fault indeed
when he stumbles behind her
onto the pavement,
feels the tiny feathers sprouting
even in his stupor of amazement.

Then the swift incredible shrinking –
pigeoning him –
into yet another pavement pigeon.
Her parting shot as she walked faster:
"Not for nothing am I Zeus' daughter."

Bette O'Callaghan
Dead Woman Walking

Always chasing love…
I was the big game hunter
stalking from continent to continent
stroking the elephant gun
dedicated to bagging the big trophy
I was the trench-coated, fedora-hatted detective
trailing love from gin joint to gin joint
down alleys and up boulevards
in every city and town I stumbled into
I was the driver on the lost highway
impelled onward by the incessant slap
of rubber on pavement, humming the siren call
of love waiting just round the next bend
I was the pirate on the sea of love
advised by a peg-legged, eye-patched parrot
to seek love's treasure at the end of the plank
I was the hippie in the summer of love
giving it up to everyone
looking for the perfect score
I was the priest at the altar of love
preaching the gospel of
you're nobody till somebody loves you
I was the dead woman walking
eating each solitary meal as if it were my last
till I chose the get out of jail free card
and flipped the bird to love

Bette O'Callaghan

Promises

Would you die for me baby?
I whispered in his ear
needed to know
he'd love me to death
forever and longer
No, he said, but I'll kill you for love
that was good enough for me

Owen O'Neill
Schoolbag

It was the first leather thing I can remember
all big buckles and resilient hard newness
with brass rivets and stitching and everything
fitting into itself with nothing left to spare
shiny on the outside and dull on the inside
like a brown horse's ear.

My schoolbag was too big for me, knocking
at my shins, the two of us full of emptiness
on our first day, but coming home proud at
three o'clock with Janet and John and a jotter.
I was soon to grow into it, learn to love it. It
would become my protector, weighed down

with the hard spines of Joyce and Hardy and
Steinback whirling through the air at my enemies
a windmill of lethal knowledge that would bust
your head wide open. It was a goalpost when a
spontaneous game of football would last into the
dark days of an echoey winter

and all we were really left kicking was a piece of
freedom away from home and work, even in that
country blackness I knew it was mine, picking it
out immediately from all the others, like a blind
man feeling a face. I learned to wear it well, broke
it down like a bucking bronco until it buckled more

»

easily and lay gently on my side. Forty years on
and the smell of leather, no matter what it is, is
always my schoolbag, sour hawthorn black ink
woody pencil shavings, rubbers tired of rubbing
and the crumbs of stale bread and education. It was
all the real learning I ever had inside that bag.

They are vanishing now, leather schoolbags.
Cyberspace and screens are the future, easily
carried and soon forgotten. I saw one the other day
in a junk shop, circa 1960. I bought it, clutched it
to my heart, and some day when I'm very old
and disappeared, they will find me, wandering in
my pyjamas, on the hard shoulder, swinging my
schoolbag, ready for a fight.

Owen O'Neill

Sick Poem

for Adrian Mitchell: "My songs may be childish as paper planes but
they glide, so thanks a lot" – his response to a critic who claimed his
poems were as childish as paper planes

A poem, stretched to its limits
Lay dying
It was as white as a sheet
No one knew what to do

Everybody gathered around
And stared
But not one person offered a word of comfort
Not one

At that precise moment
A child just happened
To be passing
I am still on duty, the child said

I will do what I can.
Picking up the poem, the child scanned it
Very carefully
Then folded it neatly into an aeroplane

And sent it off soaring
Into flight
Shouting
There, there, that poem's all right.

Rachel Pantechnicon

The Three Coalscuttles
by RACHEL PANTECHNICON

Here are the Three Coalscuttles: Coaly on the left, Scuttly in the middle, and Anthracite Lil on the end, there.

Here they are, to the left of the hearth (or fireplace).

And what they do is, when the house is quiet,

and the family have gone to bed, the Three Coalscuttles move slightly. Now they're on the right of the hearth.

And nobody knows what they're doing, except Monty the Dog. Here he is, getting their measure.

2

But Monty the Dog isn't telling.

3

And when the Three Coalscuttles have finished moving,

they go to sleep and dream about coal.

Rachel Pantechnicon

Claxton Earcaps *

I used to wear a Claxton Earcap
clapped-on, clamped-on the side of my head.
How did the slogan go?
"Claxton Earcaps keep your ears flat,
flatter than flat, in fact,
flatter than that."
Elastic contraption of pivots and pulleys,
fully functional if flattening ears
is the function you want.
"Keep still, Rachel, it won't hurt you,"
said my mother, standing on my neck
for extra leverage. "Anyway,
remember, suffering's a virtue."

And I wasn't the only one:
all us little girls in Claxton Earcaps
running round the playground
looking like Amelia Earhart in her flying helmet.
Which, when we thought about it,
made them kind of fashionable,
made us glad we needed one –
even girls with normal ears
soon pleaded with their mums to get one.
And of course it wasn't long before
Amelia Earhart herself,
always one eye on those main, main chances,
started marketing her own brand
of ear-correcting harness:
Earhart's Earcaps – grinning picure on the box –
"Amelia Earhart says, *If my ears stuck out
then I wouldn't be able to do the things I do,
like flying over the Pacific
(because of the wind resistance)."*

»

And it wasn't long before her principal foe,
her principal rival, Amy Johnson
brought a rival brand out,
cheaper and in many ways inferior.
Like the blue space-hoppers with the different faces,
no one wanted one:
they clogged up bargain bins for years to come.
Yes, Amy Johnson Earcaps were for girls
whose families were poor.

* Claxton Earcaps was commissioned as part of the Faltered States
performance project (2003), in which Apples & Snakes and the Science
Museum asked five artists to visit the Museum's private collections
and write about the objects they found there.

Brian Patten

His First Love

Falling in love was like falling down the stairs
Each stair had her name on it
And he went bouncing down each one like a tongue-tied lunatic
One day of loving her was an ordinary year
He transformed her into what he wanted
And the scent of her
Was the best scent in the world
Fourteen she was fourteen
Each day the telephone
Each day an e-mail
Each day he text her
Each day was unfamiliar
Scary even
And the fear of her going weighed on him like a stone
And when he could not see her for two nights running
It seemed a century has passed
And meeting her and staring at her face
He knew he would feel as he did forever
Hopelessly in love
Sick with it
And not even knowing her second name yet
It was the first time
The best time
A time that would last forever
Because it was new
Because he was ignorant it could ever end
It was endless

Brian Patten
Interview with a Mythical Creature

Tell me about your paw?

My paw?

I see it is bleeding.

I trod on a nail.

Not on a thorn – You didn't tread on a thorn from a rose perhaps?

No, I trod on a nail. An old nail, dropped by Noah.

So you've been around a long time?

A century is only a day seen in a different light.

A different light?

A non-egocentric light.

Too true. Describe yourself for the benefit of our readers.

No.

No?

No, I wish to remain a mystery. A description would bog down my essence.

But your paw…?   »

The one that bleeds or the one that burns?

The one that bleeds. You cannot remain a complete mystery when we know you have a paw that bleeds.

If you knew absolutely nothing about me there would be no mystery to begin with. The paw is an essential part of the myth.

Tell me, what are you doing here?

Here?

In 21st century London. Surely a myth would be more at home in ancient Greece?

I am a very small myth. As you can see I am hardly larger than a paw. I suit the times.

Chloe Poems

Bingo Jesus

A shabby man, my creation
whose baggy shadow
dances jigs long forgotten
whose dreads seem underlit by multi-coloured neon
he beams a smile
that doesn't pinpoint memory
his face a relief map
a bumpy wrinkled journey
of everyone's encounter with breath
no stranger to death
bored of the finite wisdom
of the successful
dim and distant world weary

It's whispered he can speak in tongues, this son of me
but doesn't have much to say
that he can walk on water
but there's no way he'd be reduced to parlour tricks
for poets and storytellers
hungry to be remembered.
He's offended by the restrictions of longevity
and thinks
immortality blinks
for time wasters.

For Bingo Jesus
holy water is methylated spirit
spirit that makes the miracle lights gather
a firefly disco ether   »

where he's always one step ahead
of the flautists
a favourite of tourists and children
whose giggles he knows
may one day mimic
the shortcomings of his chest
he's the best at this street theatre
of polystyrene tea and sympathy
of unintelligent bourgeois empathy
and broken tambourines.

Vanessa Richards
Slim Metal Hook

With a slim metal hook
I loop string into lace
Into light cover for June
When you are expected

I hook and avert my life
Hook to prepare for yours
As mine shifts
Collapses and expands
Around me
This string is rope
Anchoring to ancestors
Guiding my hands and your growth
Chain linking to future
Into this shawl
I am hooking storm clouds and tree resin
Snowdrops and river
Songs you may need
Prayers you will require

Your spell is warming
Tenderness huge and brutal in my chest
A moraine dislodging
A crawl of rigid tears
Shadowing this bind
Of single stitch, double stitch
Skip two
Add one

Still
Uneasy to want you so much   »

Awe
At permission
To love like this
Strain
To quell the disquiet
The journey will go wrong
Or you will change
Your watery mind
About coming to
Us
To this family
To this place
When happiness is not promised
But we are willing

With best intention
Without pattern
My Aunt Vanessa
Aunty Ness
Aunt Van
Hands hook to shield
Hook to shelter
Your fragile
Magnificence
Growing in the belly of my brother's new wife
A hothouse for you most exquisite human bloom

Naval string and cotton string
Your Mama and I are linked with blood now
And we welcome you into this kaleidoscope of kin

In your honour
I proceed
With a slim metal hook
To crotchet a mantle of love
With a matching bonnet for
You.

Vanessa Richards

Brixton Winter

Between midnight
and morning
snow fell.
Between luminous
constellations
and dim earth,
clouds gathered,
shook loose

frozen rain flowers.
Whiteness blooms on
pane ledges,
clay chimneys,
birch branches,
small gardens.

I lay in a cold frame
bed atop the house,
budding into
bruised sky.

Michèle Roberts
The announcement

Le départ de ce TGV est imminent.
Slipping away from Paris, Montparnasse
Ce train est sur le point du départ.
through concrete suburbs, over agribusiness plains
Ce train, à destination de Nantes, et de Rennes
twinned corridors of half-asleep commuters
desservira aussi la Gare du Mans, où il va se diviser en deux.
jolt and unhook. Two separate destinations now.
Le Mans. Le Mans. Deux minutes d'arrêt.
The train uncouples without fuss. Unlike us.
Attention à la fermeture automatique des portes.

Roger Robinson

Suitcase

My mother tells me that for years
she has kept a packed suitcase

In her car trunk, just in case
she had to leave urgently.

The square sky-blue leather suitcase
lay nudged against the spare wheel.

I ask, what's inside? She unzips it,
and flips the top open.

There's a black and white picture
of my sister and me when we were

eight and six, wearing white,
matching vests and shorts,

my sister is crying and I
wear an afro with a side part.

There are four white Marks and Spencer,
size thirty-two C bras, still in their box.

A smooth black leather copy of a New
Testament Bible, vacuum-packed.

Two lemon scented candles
and an orange torch light.   »

A yellowed birth certificate and a marriage
certificate slightly torn where it's creased.

An aquamarine toothbrush and onbe
dark maroon Fashion Fair lipstick.

A wooden hairbrush with stiff bristles.
An address book with her mother,

brothers' and sisters' addresses
and numbers written in red.

Twenty white airmail envelopes
with red and blue striped borders.

And recycled brown writing paper
flecked with purple flower petals.

This is all she needed.

Roger Robinson

The Ex Picture

On that murky midwinter day
your girlfriend walks slowly
towards you, brandishing
a picture of your ex-girlfriend,

asking why you still kept
her tucked between
your important documents,
in the cracked leather holdall,

perched neatly between your birth
certificate and your passport.
You try to pretend that you didn't
know where she found it.

She asks you if you're still
in love with her, and you dismiss
her with a blunt, "Of course not!"
"Prove it then," she says. "Tear it up."

You hold her in your hands
and slowly rip through, twice,
and throw it in the bin
and continue to wash the dishes.

Was it then that you learned
to sacrifice your feelings for someone
else's? Did you begin to know
how being tested felt? If you spoke

up would she hear sadness?
At certain angles the light,
shimmering off the tape,
still obscures her face.

Michael Rosen

I think I know why cats eat grass. Something
to do with them knowing that all's not well
in their guts. So they eat grass, which makes
them sick. Then, whatever it was that was
making them unwell has gone. It's not inside
anymore. It's outside. Evacuated. This is
not the same as the hair ball. Eating their own
hair also makes them sick but that's because
they lick themselves. The hair just goes in.
What I don't know is why cats put the sick
where they put it. They bring it to our doorstep.
You can tell which sick is from grass-eating
and which from hair. The grass-eating sick is
a pool of foamy sticky stuff with bits of chewed
grass in it. The hair-ball sick is more solid.
Food mixed in and held together by a wadge of
hairs. That way you can tell which of the cats
has done it. So, some of the hairy sick is ginger.
As the sun dries it and the rain washes it, we're
left with a skein of ginger hair. Like the twist
of wool you find on barbed wire when sheep
have pushed through. The mystery, though,
is why the cats want to bring us their sick. It
feels so like an offering, an act of kindness or
generosity. But that doesn't seem likely. When
you watch a cat being sick, it looks like they're
trying to bring up their whole system. Anything   »

could come out. A kidney maybe. Is it a way
of saying they hate us? We sick on you and
all that you stand for. Or maybe they think we're
Mummy and they just do things like being sick
when they're round Mummy. Because deep
inside they know that Mummy will clear it up,
give them more dinner and lick them all over.
Either that or just doing what you do with
good friends. You can do anything with good
friends. If you were at a football match and you
wet yourself, a good friend wouldn't stand up
and shout, "Hey look, my friend's wet himself."
He would just nod and say, "Yeah, right. Yeah,
I do that sometimes." Even if he didn't. Bearing
that in mind, I just want to say that the cats
are OK. They're good to be with. And that sick
thing. I didn't mean to draw too much attention to
it. I do it myself sometimes.

Jacob Ross

A Quiet Time

for Mamin

She'd come in from a long walk down one of those country roads whose thickly-plaited verge of gorse and wild grass spilled over onto the narrow strip of asphalt that seemed to lead to nowhere. Her sister and the youth weren't aware of her arrival, or if they were, they didn't seem to care. All bone and snaking muscles, the boy could have been asleep except for slow and random shifting of his hips.

They were on the large beechwood table in the space they called the kitchen: Muriel with her dress on, but rolled over her gleaming thighs, and that youth with the waist of his trousers forming a sort of bracket beneath the tensed muscles of his backside, making love in a way that sent her scuttling back out the door.

She'd stepped back into the late Normandy afternoon, her feet taking her past brown, shaven fields, dead bracken and limp, sun-struck flowers.

It was the same road that had brought them here – through the salted air and fish-renk of Dieppe, past straw-thatched villages that flew by in an ochre smear – with barely a moment to register the astonished gazes of their inhabitants, whom they jokingly referred to as the *natives*.

She'd even imagined herself above the car – a paraglider perhaps, or the hot metallic eye of the sun looking down on three nappy heads leant back against the peach-pink leather seats of Muriel's saffron-coloured Mercedes SL350. A firefly on wheels, curving a bright flaming arc from the outskirts of Rouen to that little wooden building in the middle of a field.

Only once did the gendarmes turn their eyes on them. Somewhere between Paris and Rouen, a flashing Citroen drew up close, ran parallel with them while cubic zirconia eyes took in the alloy-rimmed wheels of the car, its curving lines, the British number plates, and then scanned their faces, pausing over Muriel and the dozy, long-boned boy before coming to rest finally on her and staying there.

She knew what they were looking at; had grown accustomed to it by now: her bottle-smooth almost purple darkness that *her* Toni, Toni of the knowing hands and querying lips, had taught her to be proud of; the hair cropped close to her skull, large egg-yolk-white eyes; or just the length and reach of her, which – before her limbs had straightened out and the gangle turned to grace – had so appalled her in her pre-teens.

She'd turned her head, held the driver's eyes and smiled. The pale face softened. The man showed his teeth briefly, then, alarmed at himself it seemed, he shouted something above the thunder of the engines and the car angled away from them like a fish slipping into the traffic of the slower lane.

"What'd he say?" Muriel wanted to know.

"Salut or salope," Kisha chuckled loudly.

The youth shifted his weight in the seat, sucked in his lower lip and went back to sleep.

"Likes what he saw, I s'pose!" Muriel looked at her appraisingly in the mirror and smiled. "That dress really suits you, girl. I wore it once and wondered why the hell I wasted so much money on that thing. It was a good idea to take the collar off."

Leaning back, she'd pushed an arm outside the window and the vehicle surged forward, chewing up the asphalt as if it were a never-ending strip of gum.

They'd arrived finally at that old converted barn perched on a small rise in the middle of a wide, dishevelled field that seemed to go on forever.

* * * *

She had returned to the little house tired and light-headed with the things she'd discovered, especially the small, tree-covered hill at the bottom of the road which stood out dark and ragged like a Rasta's head against the bleached-out sky. She'd spotted it the evening of their first day there, climbed its slope the next day and gazed down on the cows, the farms, the small flower-covered village just beyond and the road that looped around it like a noose.

A diffuse headache pulsed at the back of her eyes now. She hadn't eaten anything since morning. And she couldn't think of anything worthwhile to do. Didn't know how long those two were going to be back there. Thought that she might as well climb that hill again, sit on the large round stone up there and try to clear her mind.

With a small eddy of outrage, she brought her foot down on a snail. Felt it crumble beneath her boot with the crackling of popcorn. She watched it squirm and die at the end of its own semen-like trail and thought that if all this *holiday* was going to be was being witness to her sister's goings-on with that boy, she might as well have stayed in London.

And then it crossed her mind that she should expect that Muriel and her man, together, in a place so far removed from anywhere, would make this time for themselves.

She did not like it, though. Did not like the quiet turbulence in her guts, the deep-down flaring of her nerves which, even here on this footpath, turned her mind reluctantly to the butterflies copulating on the edge of stalks, the man-smell of dried grass, the rank of bulls in the fields that rolled away from her towards that little postcard village.

This was not what Muriel had hinted at when she last called. A quiet time, she'd said. A quiet time in Normandy in what used to be a farmhouse. It was a present from her for the big favour that she, Kisha, had done for her.

It was Muriel's thirteenth call in two weeks. Before that she hadn't heard from her sister in three years.

She'd wanted to pretend she didn't know the voice. Didn't recognise that tone – filed down, buffed and polished until there was no evidence of the real person behind it. No trace of who she was or where she came from. She wanted to say, "Hello, Muriel Martin," hold her breath on *that* surname; fill it with the bits of acid that Muriel's tone stirred up in her. Instead she'd queried quietly, "Y'awright, Sis?"

Muriel didn't even seem to hear her.

"Kish! Kish, Girrrrl – Kisha, you there?" She sounded as excited and conspiratorial as though they'd been girl-talking everyday.

"Uh-huh."

"Girrrrl, I found a man."

"Found?"

"Yep," and I'm going to keep this one."

"Christ, the way you talk sometimes."

Muriel chuckled: short, musical, throaty. "Want to say hello?" Her voice hollowed and faded into a string of background chirpings.

"No," she said, surprised. "He there?"

Muriel chuckled again.

"Serious?"

"Mmmm-hmm!"

"Um, how old?"

The briefest of silences, as if Muriel had paused to catch her breath. "Does it matter?"

"How old, Muriel?" She was smiling into the phone. Was glad Muriel couldn't see her.

"Well, you know the saying: wimmen stay stronger longer..."

Kisha could hear the metal creeping into the voice at the other end. "Uh-huh?"

"Twenty in ten month's time. Somming wrong with that?"

"No, not at all."

"Okay. Friday then. Just the three of us. At Books Etc? The Angel? They've got a decent cafe upstairs. Eight alright with you?"

"Hang on, Muriel."

"Whatsimatter, Sunshine. Don't you want to see me?"

"Did I say that? And don't call me Sunshine. You don't expect..."

"It's important, Kisha. Besides, don't forget you owe me. Eight o'clock then!"

"Murie, hey!"

Muriel had hung up.

* * * *

She'd found herself there an hour or so before them. She'd spent longer than she usually did in front of the mirror. She'd ironed her best top and the Ted Baker jeans she'd spotted in an Oxfam shop in Wood Green. And though partial to silver, she'd passed half a morning rummaging for the gold chain Toni had bought her for their Valentine. She'd even swapped her large silver hoops for a borrowed pair of emerald studs.

Oddly, on her perch on the stool above the square from which she could see the hundreds of milling heads below, her eyes fell on the youth first. He looked like any other lean-limbed young man on the street, with loose army-green trousers and trainers designed to draw attention to his feet. Clean-cropped, as if he'd just emerged from the barber's. Maybe it was the crisp white shirt at a time when creases and hoods were all the rage that drew her eyes to him. Perhaps it was his walk: that easy, loose-limbed stride, with his head and shoulders following through with every step he took, almost as if he were drifting. Maybe it was all of that pulled together that made it clear to her that he was foreign: West Indian. And just arrived.

Muriel walked beside him like one of those women taking her charge to the funfair for the first time. She looked like money. A charcoal-grey, loose-fitting suit that yielded with every swing of those jangling brown arms. She'd swept her hair back from her forehead like a cobra's cowl. Sashayed across the cobbles with black Gucci shoes so highly polished, they appeared silver in the daylight. For no reason she could put a finger on, Kisha felt her breathing quicken.

"Hello, girrrl." Muriel gurgled, eyes bright. Smile tight. They exchanged frank, assessing gazes.

Muriel was nearing the age when the struggle with the body really started; when the veins at the back of the hand began their push against the skin. It was all there: the barely discernible loosening of the flesh at base of the throat, the face slowly surrendering its shape to the bones beneath, the hair at the base of the temples just slightly lighter than the rest. Over the three years that she hadn't seen her sister, time had been speeding up for Muriel. And it would take a lot more time for her to accept that no amount of creaming, honey or money could put a brake on it. This was the time when the Muriels of this world dressed up a little more provocatively, made a religion of colours that hid or niced-up their shape, became mathematicians overnight from calculating calories, put a lot more value on the admiration in a man's gaze. You learned these things from working five days a week for six years in a hairdressing salon on Stoke Newington High Street.

"Looking good," Muriel told her, smiling.

"You too," she nodded. And she meant it. Muriel was still lovely to look at. A person would have to look real hard to see the things she'd just observed. Her sister had always made much of her loaf-brown skin; her long and not-so-very-black hair and eyes, and that nose which she said, on the authority of her research on the Internet, she'd traced all the way back to ancient Syria.

It turned out that Muriel had not so much met the youth as saved him.

"I spent my hols this year in Jamaica. Had to sort out some things over there for Mother." Muriel glanced down at her nails and threw a vacant look across the cafeteria. "She talks about you more and more these days, you know."

"Anyhow, I saw Rikky from my window. He was up against this hotel fence, near the beach, you know; and three big guys were kicking the shite out of him. One of them was trying to slash his face or something. God – these people… they're so *violent!*" Muriel opened disbelieving eyes at her.

"He gave as good as he got though. In fact better. I've never seen anything like it, Keesh. I made the hotel call the police. He came over to thank me afterwards. That's how..." Muriel swivelled her head at Rikky and threw him a girlish grin. The young man smiled back.

He hardly spoke. Before they sat down, Muriel had simply told her, her lashes fluttering like butterflies, "That's mah maaaaen, Keesh. Say hello, Rikky!" and he'd got up from the table she'd pointed him to, taken her hand and said hello in a voice that had caught her unawares. It seemed too deep to belong to him, too rich and ripe for someone as baby-faced as he. It was as if he'd borrowed an older man's throat.

Muriel held her eyes and dropped her voice almost to a whisper, "Rikky's here on holiday and he's not going back."

Kisha nodded neutrally.

"I, I'm asking you a favour, Keesh." Muriel was leaning into her face.

"Go on, den."

Muriel sat back, tried to smile, tried to hold her eyes. Gave up and focused on her chin.

"Well – I'm asking you to marry him. For me."

Muriel had lost the Nat West voice, the Loans Manager intonations which she'd cultivated for so long that they had become first nature. She was now Muriel of the loose, uncertain mouth, of the nervous hand that wandered to her throat and stayed there.

"Sorry?"

"I'll, I'll uhm – pay you, if that's..."

Kisha placed the cup of coffee down so gently she scarcely heard it touch the table. She found herself leaning across it towards Muriel. "That's what you asked me to come here for? Uh? That's why you phoned me after three years? Three years – and you two haven't even bothered to find out if I'm dead or living in shit. Not once. In three years! And then you call me outta the blue. You ask me to meet you here. For what? To ask me this?"

"I'm offering to..."

"Hold it right there! Don't go no further." She'd lifted a hand and levelled a finger at Muriel's face. A thin film of sweat had forced its way through Muriel's makeup.

"You haven't changed. That temper of yours still *so* nasty." She said it softly, without reproach. "I thought time might have, well… made things a bit better, y'know. Look, you're thinking it's the job. It's not. Not just that. It's a couple of other things..."

"Like what?"

"It's not a favour I'm asking, y'know. I'm offering to…"

"Like what, Muriel?"

Muriel would not look at her. She cast a quick, furtive glance over at the youth. Now she looked slightly frightened.

"Shane," she muttered, her voice a whisper. "Remember Shane?"

Kisha remembered him: too much chat, too much curly-perm and so much gold round his wrists and neck, he was like a walking pawnshop. "That one. Flash Pants."

"You never liked him."

Kisha twisted her mouth and shrugged.

"After you, well… left. Well, you weren't around anymore. A few things happened. Me and Shane, we sort of decided to, y'know…"

Kisha narrowed her eyes and leaned forwards suddenly. "You married that, that bloke – that's it? That right? You *actually*… Christ! And it didn't even cross your mind to take up the phone and call to say, 'Dog, I'm getting married'? How long it last – coupla weeks? Did it? And now you're in a twist, coz…"

"It wasn't like that. Jeezus, Kisha – you make it sound so *crude*!"

Kisha laughed. The boy lifted his head and stared at them.

"You want me to beg. Okay I'll…"

"Sort it out yourself, Muriel."

"I can't. I really wish… It's only for a year, you know. He'll stay with me. You do it. I'll sort myself out, you divorce and then…"

"No."

"For God's sake, we're supposed to be sisters!"

"Don't even try that! Y'hear me? Don't!"

Muriel dragged her handbag to her. Her fingers hovered above the mouth. "How much is it worth to you, Kisha? Tell me. A grand? A couple? Three? Just tell me." Muriel's stare was hard and accusing.

"Uh-uh."

Muriel pulled her feet together and got up, creating a small eddy of perfume around her.

"You got a short memory," she breathed. "That's all I can to say."

"Quite the opposite, actually. Reminding me again of the time you saved my arse?"

"C'mon, Rikky." The youth had spread his upper half almost flat on the table. He'd been examining his hands.

"I'll phone," Muriel muttered, barely turning to glance at Kisha. "You still *owe* me, y'know."

She watched them leave before digging into her pocket and pulling out some coins. She gave them half an hour, got to her feet and walked out onto the High Street. The day was crisp and bright – the pre-summer kind that made her want to pull her collar close – but not cold enough for gloves.

She stared speculatively at the entrance to the busy Shopping Centre and, with a chuckle and a sigh, decided to do some window-gazing.

* * * *

...You still owe me...

Muriel kept saying that. And a time *must* come when she would have to set her straight. Not that she could ever forget what Muriel kept referring to. But over the years, she'd stuffed that night in '99 somewhere in a back drawer in her mind. That night before the Carnival when they'd decided to burn out the hours in an all-night rave in Camden and carry the party mood with them to Notting Hill.

The girls they'd come with were kicking up a storm in one corner of the hall. Muriel was misbehaving like a drunk on steroids, although she never drank. She and Muriel, they both had that in common.

Kisha had spliffed out before entering the black-walled building and drifted into her own little purple haze, shifting on the rhythm whenever she felt like it, and smiling back at the storm out there. She was sharing the mood with a yout'man who'd floated across to her side. He didn't say hello. Just looked at her briefly in her face, smiled as if answering to something she'd been thinking and picked up her rhythm with his arms and legs. He was as tall as she and clearly on a similar kind of high.

A couple of hours later, she couldn't even remember if they'd even spoken, they stepped out together. Nothing heavy. Not even talking. Just to take in the chill out there because with that kinda high she knew it would feel like mint on the skin. She was kind of amazed too that they'd met up in there in the eye of a hurricane rave and had found each other floating on the same wave.

Nothing would have come of it though. She was sure of that. Not a single thing.

The trouble came from behind her – a thick, pink-haired woman, a brawler in red jeans that clung to her ham-sized calves like lycra, with the fists of a boxer and a mouth as wide and raucous as a bin, had grabbed herself a fistful of *her* hair, spun her round and started to 'buse her. She could still see that face: thick and tight and glistening with hatred. Abuse her because her man had decided to step outside with her to take some flippin' fresh air. Make matters worse she was brandishing a knitting pin or something in her hand. With intent!

Without pausing to draw breath, Kisha reached out, smashed her knuckles in Bin-Mouth's eyes and, before the girl could steady herself, she'd followed up with a boot in her gut. It was later, after the police came, that Muriel found out that the girl was pregnant.

She'd left the scene by then, her legs taking her along the snort and snore of King's Cross, all the way down to the South Bank. It had taken her at least a couple of hours to get there. She was three hours out there in the cold on a bridge above the Thames before heading home. When she got there, Muriel was parked outside her flat. She'd stayed behind to "check out the drama," she said. And when the police asked, she'd said she'd never seen the 'assailant' before. But one of Miss Red Jeans' girlfriends had described her in detail, Muriel said. Especially the way she had her hair. Got it down to a T; even the way she'd sewn the silver threads through it. And it was true that, throughout that night and even the days that followed, it seemed to her that the city was full of police sirens. Muriel helped her pull out the silver threads and she, fearful even to step out, sat in her flat for almost a month while Muriel brought her the things she needed.

It was Muriel's idea to cut it off. The hair that even her sister used to look at with some amazement, for it was thick and strong and raven black. It never moulted. It never thinned or dried or cracked. The kind of hair that bounced back from the assault of everything she'd ever thrown at it: hot combs, creams and gels and perms. She'd curled it, twisted it, clipped it, snipped it, tressed it and distressed it. And in those times when things had been really bad with her, she'd neglected it completely – sometimes for a year.

It was the first thing her girlfriends touched when they examined her. And without so much as asking, they knew how she was doing by the way she had her hair.

Now here was Muriel urging her to cut it off.

It made sense though, because she'd had it all gelled up and carved and scooped around her head with silver threads running through for highlights. At that party her hair was as obvious as a road sign.

Muriel did the job herself. She'd never seemed so careful about anything. So thorough. And at the end of it, she stood back, the scissors in her fist, staring at her baldness in the mirror, a half-smile softening her mouth, a look of wonderment quivering in her eyes. That and something else that in all these years Kisha could never put a name to.

Perhaps it was that she wanted to preserve: the odd mixture of self-doubt and God-knows-what-else on Muriel's face as they both stared at the hair that had descended in a thick black nightfall to the floor. Perhaps she wanted to hold onto the sureness of those fingers, the ease with which they'd slipped above her scalp. But she'd never felt the urge to grow it back.

And now she'd grown into her semi-baldness, had even learnt to like it. Because people looked at her, checked themselves and then looked again. A certain type of person would even try to catch her eye. And if it were a man, he would never hold her gaze for long.

* * * *

The headache had taken over completely by the time she decided to return. Muriel was sunning herself out on the sloping bit of grass that passed for a back garden, her loose flowered dress drawn up to her knees.

The young man was stretched out on a long plastic chair beside her, his eyes covered with one arm. They'd brought out a bottle of Calvados – presumably for him – and a small basket stuffed with baguettes, cheeses, slices of veal, and the foie gras that he'd taken a liking to.

"Want something?" Muriel queried sweetly.

"Sorry?"

"You hungry?" Muriel gestured at the basket.

"Uh-uh."

Kisha sat slightly behind her and stared out across the fields. From here, she could see the houses that these sprawling fields supported. A sunset like a bale of kente cloth spread itself above their heads. She watched waves of quarrelling birds drift across it, their wings scribbling darkly against all that glow and shine.

The air was chock-a-block with sounds she couldn't identify, apart from the far-off hum and thud of farm people preparing themselves for retreat into their flower-covered cottages.

These little houses were a far cry from the tall, indifferent boxes that stood above Hackney's streets. In fact, from here, after just three days, London felt like that too, an unreal and distant Legoland which, in this heat, had disintegrated to a cotton-woolly vagueness in her mind. Even Toni, whom she used to wait for on her sofa, a bottle of Baileys, which they never shared, getting turbo-chilled in the freezer, was more sensation than shape now.

She imagined Toni lying on some woman's floor now, teaching her the things she'd also been taught, showing her how little she knew her body.

"Whyd'ju bring me here, Muriel?"

"You mean, why did you accept my invitation?"

Muriel fingered her dark glasses up to the top of her forehead and rolled her eyes back towards her. "That's what you been asking yourself?"

"Well... not like that... but..."

"But what?"

"Well – perhaps I'm being silly. But I didn't expect it to be so, sort of, well... y'know – so..."

"So?"

"Well, tight – I mean, *closed*. We've been here three days and it's not as if it's just the two of you here. We don't talk. We don't eat together; we don't go check out the place together. Just this... this… dunnoh, man! A little bit of…" She wanted to say *respect* or perhaps *consideration* but they sounded more appropriate in her head than if she were to say them.

Muriel took her glasses off and levelled steady brown eyes at her. "You're talking and I'm not understanding, because you're not *telling* me anything. What you getting at, Sunshine?"

It was the Nat West voice. Kisha hunched her shoulders as if bracing herself against it.

"You didn't have to come, you know."

"You asked me, didn't you?"

"And I didn't have to, Keesh. That's the point I'm making, because I'd already paid you."

Muriel replaced her Ray Bans on her forehead, her mouth tensing in a mock half-smile. "Eight more days to go, Sunshine. Better learn to live with it."

Kisha surprised herself by smiling. This, she thought, was the real Muriel. The one who tied you up so tight you didn't have a free arm to even scratch yourself with.

They were in a converted barn somewhere between Forges-les-Eaux, and Neufchatel and a good few miles from Dieppe. That was all she'd taken the time to register.

Something shifted itself in her head suddenly. It lifted the head-ache nibbling at the tissue behind her forehead and made her look about her as if she'd just arrived.

"Going to catch a nap," she said, and left them there.

* * * *

She'd taken the room next door, a coffin of a space with a single mattress thrown over a sort of palette made from rough board. Muriel and the youth had taken the bigger room.

From this small room, their tossings filled her nights: the growling of the youth, like the bulls that stood and stared at her out there; Muriel's sighs, her pleasure-sobs slipping easily into giggles, so that the whole night became a kind of stew in which those two rolled roughshod over her sleep. She would finally drift off, but when she woke up in the morning, her body felt as if it had been soaked and spun and tumble-dried.

She now knew that all of this was meant for her. Another woman would have pushed her away, done all the little, nasty, upsetting things – the way a landlord would force a tenant out without uttering a word – to keep her from 'distracting' her man. Not Muriel. She needed some-thing more. Had to bring her here, grab her by the back of the head and bury her face so deeply in it, she couldn't even breathe.

And for some reason, these two were succeeding in pushing her back, back to remembering a little, bitter woman, scalpel-tongued and dark as she, who'd never said a word to her without a sneer, whose eyes syringed her with a million awful statements. They were taking her back to *that* time in *that* school above the Hackney Marshes, to a girl named Tracy Whitlow who used to puzzle her because she used to be so desperate for her friendship. Tracy Whitlow was all she could remember of Clapton Comprehensive – apart from the stink of the fumes from the traffic at the roundabout that they could literally lean over and spit onto. Tracy Whitlow swirling her doll-soft hair about her face... Tracy Whitlow talking, talking till kingdom come about her boyfriend who loved her creamy stomach and the little corn-yellow hairs there. Until she, dark, fleshless, and gangle-limbed like a cloth doll, felt herself in some quiet, unnameable way, being gradually reduced.

Tracy had taught her one important thing; that within the folds of friendship, there often slept the seeds of a very quiet violence.

* * * *

Mornings, she would take the track that led to the little mound in the middle of the fields she now called Rasta Hill and spend an hour there. Sometimes longer. When she returned, Muriel was already out on her own 'personal time,' which was really a joy-ride through the sleeping country lane that led out of the village. She would sometimes catch sight of the top of the car gliding like a bright metallic insect amongst the tall hedgerows.

Lately though, she didn't feel like taking a walk of any kind. She would have a light breakfast, or rather pick at the grapes and bits of cheese and bread; place finger-daubs of raspberry jam on her tongue along with dollops of fiery mustard which felt like small explosions in her mouth and nostrils. Enjoying the sensation more than she did the food.

With Muriel gone, the youth seemed to take up no space. He sat at the table, his legs hidden in its shadow, his hands on the wooden surface, his head slightly down as if he were studying his fingers, so that all she could see were the lids of his eyes. It was as if he'd put all the life in him on hold. Didn't even seem to be awaiting Muriel's return.

This was someone who moved only when he had to, she decided, who kept what he wanted hidden behind those half-shut lids, who had mastered the trick of biding time. Toni had said that about her once.

And yet Muriel said he was a 'street bwoy' – one of those youths who'd learned to use a knife before he knew how to walk. His hands, she noticed, were like his voice. They did not belong to him. They were older than his face, older than his age. She saw that Muriel hadn't got to his nails yet. Wouldn't be able to do much about the scarred thumb or those high-ridged tendons at the back of his hands, which switched like cables and gave those spidery fingers a life of their own.

She wasn't aware exactly when she began asking him to do things, even if she'd been counting the days and there were just three more to go. First it was to fetch a cup for her which he rinsed before he handed over. Then it was to put the kettle on, which also required him to fetch the matches, light the stove, fill it and place it on the hob. Single requests that required of him a whole series of movements. To pull the window shut he needed to unwind his legs, straighten himself out of the chair, cross the floor and stretch his full length up to reach the catch. And it was the same to move the heavy, rough-log table a little further from the wall.

His strength seemed almost casual, and like his voice and hands, it seemed to have no connection with his body. He simply did what she ordered without a single utterance.

Maybe it was because she wanted to see him move – to catch a glimpse of the life that he was being so careful to conceal even from Muriel. Something of the intent and the danger she thought she saw in those 'knifeman's' hands.

When it came, it was with a chuckle and a quiet drawl that caught her off-guard and sent a shiver down the skin of her arms.

"Why you doan come out wid it," he said.

"Sorry?"

"You waant me. But you doan know how fe say it."

"Pardon?"

"Y'hear me firs time."

With a jerk of her hand, she knocked the cup off the wooden table. It hit the stone floor and fragmented like a small grenade. She felt the hot liquid on her feet and winced. His trouser ends were soaked too but he didn't move an inch.

"What the hell? How dare you?"

"Me not wrong. Me never wrong bout dese tings." He stated it as fact.

"My God! What kind of person are you?"

"Me do what me haffe do." Now the voice belonged entirely to him. His eyes were directly on hers, the long face hard and angular, his gaze not threatening, just quiet and assessing.

"Muriel's not simply a friend, you know; she's my sister!"

"Wha mek she hate you so much den?"

"That's crap. She told you that?"

He chuckled, as if at something private. "It doan have no love between you two."

She found she could not look at him.

The throbbing of Muriel's engine reached them. On hearing the vehicle, the youth's shoulders lowered. A sort of limpness came over him, almost as if he were pulling on another garment. She shook her head as if to clear her vision, and stepped out for her walk.

* * * *

With Muriel out there mid-mornings, burning rubber on the road, the youth would make two cups of coffee and hand her one. Sometimes he would place a bowl of grapes before her, still dripping with tap water. He said nothing. Neither did she. And even if Muriel's arrival had cut short their confrontation, somehow if felt as if their conversation had been complete.

She'd imagined him following her out there, the awkward conversation, the ugly slug of words which, despite their challenge and abuse, would make it easier for her. But he was there before her, on her stone, in one of those sleeveless T-shirts he'd arrived in.

He'd drawn his knees up to his chin, arms straight out behind him. Just a shape against the bleached-out sky so that he looked like an oversized 'N' perched on the massive 'O' of the stone. And with a start she realised that he must have followed her to this place before.

His presence made the place feel different. She noticed for the first time the hints of rust in the purple moss that covered the sloping earth, the patch of darkness just beyond them, where the lower branches of the trees tied themselves together in a sort of cave, the hollow humming of the land beyond her that a person felt rather than heard. And she knew that she would never want to set foot on this hill again.

He smelt of the meat he'd been feeding on every day, and of the fierceness with which she let him take her. He was too confident, too sure of his effect on her for it to be any good. There was neither ugliness nor pleasure there for her. Just fact. And near the end, when his body began to tense into a single, living shudder, and his brows and mouth were softening into a child's, she arched herself high and hard and threw him off.

He was still gasping when she straightened up. Sitting on the grass as he had been when she first caught sight of him on her approach. She'd heard it said that some men, brought to that point, and abruptly let down became either violent or docile – some were even known to cry. He was neither. There was something chastened in the way he looked – not at her but at the grass between his feet.

They climbed down the hill – she leading the way. Half way down, they met the conspiratorial eyes of a short, wide man, his face brown and rugged as bark, who barely paused from swinging the small scythe at the root of the grass that he was gathering.

She wanted to say, perhaps to the man or to the youth, or the strangely humming landscape around them, that she'd never done this sort of thing before, wasn't the kind who did, never knew she had it in her and that she blamed Muriel for bringing it out of her.

As soon as their feet hit the path, she felt his hand on her arm. "You nice," he said.

With a surge of irritation, she swung her head to face him. "Can't say the same about you."

His jaw hardened. The danger she had sensed in him and which, such a short while ago, had in some way been confirmed, washed over her like a mustard bath.

"Me leave aar fi yuh." He said it softly. The urgency was in his grip.

"Why?"

"Is how me feel. Here." He touched his stomach. Where his navel would be beneath the shirt.

"Kinda quick, innit?"

"Me do wha me haffe do."

She wondered what he meant by that. Decided she knew and smiled neutrally at him.

"Well... I married you. So, technically..." She ran a hand across the prickles on her head, thinking that she would have to cut them soon. "Fact is, though, I don't want you. Never did. But you wouldn't understand that."

She thought she heard him mutter something, the tail end of which was, "crazy..." It brought a small smile to her mouth.

The car was parked almost in the doorway when they walked into the yard. Rikky was slightly behind her.

Muriel sat at the table. Her elbows were propping up her face. Kisha had a quick impression of the bulk of her, her dark solidity against the bright backlight from the window above her head. She stepped into a silence so thick, she felt as if she were wading.

Her eyes quickly scanned the space: the small basket of wild black berries and pears, the four loaves of bread that Muriel invariably brought back with her, the heavy bread knife, the handle of which was touching Muriel's elbow. The woman's heavy breathing.

"You! Get in here." Muriel's voice seemed to have erupted from her stomach. Kisha felt the young man brush past her. His hands stuffed down his pockets, he placed his back against the wall.

Muriel swung her head towards her, her lower lip pulled inward, her eyes still and bright with hatred.

"I thought you weren't into men... I thought you were a bloody..."

"Say it, Muriel! Say it: Lez? Dyke? Say it!" She felt an old and deadly anger stirring in her blood.

"That's why, *that's* why Mother threw your black arse out. Frickin' African."

Kisha leaned a shoulder against the doorway. "Senegalese,

actually," she said, her eyes fixed on the spot where Muriel's elbow touched the table. "He didn't even know she had me. She told him she wasn't going to, and then she kicked him out, yes, like she kicked me out. She told you who your father was, didn't she? She never told me mine. I found out though. Like I found out that girl – all dem years back – in that party in Camden wasn't carrying no child. And no fuckin' police came."

With quivering lips she turned her gaze fully on the boy. "Funny, Muriel, innit? The only thing we got in common. Me 'n' you. We ain't into *men*."

Muriel moved then. Like a small eruption. She grabbed the knife. Kisha stooped almost the same time and straightened up with the brick they used as a doorjamb. But the youth was already there between them. And she noticed with a quiver of disbelief that the knife was in his hand. She'd never seen a person move so quickly.

"Done it, Muriel," he said. "Me say, finish it!"

Muriel tried to fight her way past him but wherever she turned, she found him there in front of her. She struck out at him then, sobbing. The only time he dodged her swing was when she lashed out at his face. The rest he took unflinching.

And then, as if her whole body had deflated, Muriel slumped back in the chair.

Kisha dropped the brick. "He saved your life, Muriel Martin. Now you're both even. I'm getting outta this... this *barn*."

She was in the room and back out in an instant, with the bag she'd packed the night before. Muriel followed her movements as if her eyes were attached to her by a string. Kisha strode through the doorway, eased herself around the car and paused to contemplate a clutch of small birds skidding over the clean-shaven fields, and the brown crosshatch of farm roads which on her first day here, she'd likened to the lines in a head of neatly plaited hair.

The main road was ten miles or so away, perhaps further. But someone would stop for her. There would always be people, farmers or somebody passing through, who would notice her strangeness in this landscape and want to get a closer look.

She was counting on that to get her home.

Joy Russell

English Bath

England, I plunged
into your little island
dropped all the way
from JFK, New York to London, Heathrow,
Hudson to Thames, *wadah* to *watah*
– the new world to greet the old

a blue passport sweaty

at immigration, travelled the Circle
Yellow, or District Green, stepped off
to find B & B, *You lost, love?* found me
directions, a room, not quite
ready, a café to drink black

coffee white. London, with your miserable
grey, brick and brown, your golden pint
of lager louts, your fine manner of rudeness,
working-class, middle-class, from over
there-class, born-here-but-still-not-British-class, I

plunged
in

to all of your loveliness, your cruel
and wicked and delicate ways,
your bangers and mash, your puds and pies,
your slappers and your snoggers
your wankers and your woosies

»

the Thames,
        snaking
a muddy line
divide of North and South

translated: tongue split
your history –
white linen bloodied with strawberries

I plunged, sunk
deep in a hot
tub, mirror
        vanishing through fog

Joy Russell

This Time

This time,
let's talk about
you when you were alive.
I'd like that better than
this aching muscle at the back of the ear
my grief laid flat out on the table
autumn coming too soon
and this tiny drop of nostalgia heavy
on a rainy afternoon.
Yes, I'd like that.

Sometimes,
you were so impossible.
You, with your strong upper-body and
skinny-toothed legs, trailing scent that drove both
sexes wild, come-and-get-me eyes, and 'that' voice:
rough whiskey over pebbles. Yes, let's talk about
how you wore those gorgeous professor jumpers, how
your brother was a broader shorter beefier inverted
image of you. Oh yes, I'd
like that, cause it's

an afternoon of nostalgia and I've searched
everywhere in the house for my missing black T-shirt,
have gone though everybody's black wardrobe, droning on
where is it, where is it, applied orange stain across
lips, heard the nasal whine of Geraldo's tv chat show asking
Helen, how long has your hair loss problem been going on?
and *We're here today to talk about hair loss,* and I don't
give a damn, don't give a good god damn at all, except
this time, for nostalgia's sake, let's talk about
you when you were alive. I'd like that,
I really would.

Jacob Sam-La Rose

Bone

for Abe

What they want is something as indisputable
as bone. All we can give, of course,
is the soft meat of ourselves. And for us,

it's enough – we wouldn't expect to be asked
for more, although we catch ourselves
in conversation, wondering how much

it would hurt, to peel back the skin,
sculpt the flesh, trim the unnecessary parts
until we reach something close. Soon enough,

we're bruised, holding the phone too hard,
trying to fit the spaces left by the voice
at the other end of the line,

unable to recognise the sound of our own.
Guilty for wondering which organ to excise
or which is non-negotiable –

what ground is firm enough to stand,
what ground can be given.

Jacob Sam-La Rose

The End of Summer

it has seemed to me | that memory is a kind of hunger
– Robert Gibb, *Salt*

You promised you'd write,
a smile still fresh on your lips.
I neither knew nor cared for
the arithmetic of long distance.

Stepped back to fix you in memory:
the precise length of your hair, cheeks
glowing yellow from the puffed jacket you wore;
the size of your hand, fingers splayed

against mine; the narrow stretch of hall
in your apartment block where we pledged
breathless goodbyes, pressed together
dreams of next time, promises not to forget

still dancing on our tongues, underneath
the halogen hum of hall lights still burning
as if we could ignore the early morning outside,
rising, cool and inevitable, all too soon.

I would have kept everything we whispered
only, weeks later, home and half a world away,
those details began to struggle and fade.
I waited patiently for an inked kiss,

the mark of your hand on a page. Anything
that might cross the distance, set
those details singing again. Anything
to spark my recollection.

Sapphire
August 9th

for the Hibakusha, the survivors of Hiroshima and Nagasaki

Hate, black teeth, half an
eyeball, torn light, green grass, dirt
wings. Sick, blind angel.

Kadija Sesay

the moon under water

for saffi

the moon under water
curves like my sister's smile

as my sister swims under water
her form is like a smiling moon

she curves, she smiles, she beams; she
kisses the moon, under water

her essence reflects silver like the moon

Kadija Sesay

chasing thoughts

I found myself
chasing your thoughts

trying to reach the destination
of your feelings

before you had arrived there –
so that I could safely

position the fence
to stop you grabbing mine.

John Siddique
Pins and Needles

That bed, spread with colour like a Klimt kiss.
We are wrapped in cloth. Wrapped in glist.
Bound up with each other. Jigsaw pieces of arms.

You find me down the side of the couch.
You sleep hard on my chest. It only takes a minute.
Your breath in time with my heartbeat, and you sleep.

I watch and guess the light through the blind cracks.

We are wrapped in purple and gold thread.
You wanted to feel royal. My chin against your forehead.
My sleeping arm quite numb and dead, holding round your back.

Sharrif Simmons

Fuck What Ya Heard

The new J Edgar Hoover is John Ashcroft
Sitting in his office wearing red, white and blue panties
My friends ask me:
"Man… when you gonna leave all of this alone?"
Not until Mumia's home
Or Assata is safe here
I've got so little fear
And so much shit to talk
Like how they let these motherfuckers from Enron walk
Or how a governor from Texas outlined America in chalk
The election was for sale
So it got bought
And now they got us all in some deep-ass shit
Like a seven-forty-seven with Bin Laden in the cockpit
The new world order is the same old shit
Hell to the poor
Heaven for the rich
But funny how money changes a situation
Cause the same damn money fuels reparation
And you can catch it on prime time
Or HBO
So:
Fuck what ya heard
And act like you know
Fuck what ya heard
And act like you know   »

The new Kennedy
Is no one
He doesn't exist
They killed the man
The idea
The legend
The myth
The Reverend Al Sharpton
Is the new Martin Luther the King
Screaming from Washington:
"Let freedom ring"
But freedom never showed up, so we bought it with the bling
And now the new revolution is a P Diddy thing
And I ain't mad at nobody for making that dough
So:
Fuck what ya heard
And act like you know
Fuck what ya heard
And act like you know

Now making dough is all good
It's like a natural fact
But I just can't turn my back on those chosen few
Who believe everything that you see on the news
But the real controversies don't make it to the top
Like the gay underground in the world of Hip-Hop
Like the missing WMDs in the sands of Iraq
And all the mystery diseases poppin' up in the East
Like AIDS in Africa
It bears the Mark of the Beast
And at least I see the forest
through the thick of the trees that I burn
After every last one of my shows   »

So:
Fuck what ya heard
And act like you know
Fuck what ya heard
And act like you know

Now I said all of that
Just so I can say this
Remember your past, or your future will be missed
This isn't the first search for weapons in Baghdad
Gilgamesh searched for them
In the valley of the Shem
The land of the rackets is what they called it back then
He went to war with Assyrians and Babylonians with power
Over rumors of weapons and communication towers
And not long after that Ezekiel seen the fling wheel
So hold on to your caps
Cause it's about to get peeled
All this talk about Jesus coming back
Forgiving our sins and putting us on the right track...

When Jesus comes back he'll
Be on the attack with a space ship
A helmet and a big fat gat
The Catholic religion is about to collapse
From the weight of the children on all the priests' laps

And when they ask you where you heard it
You can tell 'em fo' sho:
Fuck what ya heard
And act like you know

Sharrif Simmons
The Gift

Faced with the mountain of ideas
Another nighttime ends
Another day begins

This day will be different
It will be marked and recorded as a present
A gift
The present is like a gift

Today will be scented by cooked apples, burnt cinnamon
And blue mountain coffee
Both of my suns will shine
The first one sleeps late on Saturdays
The second one comes through my kitchen window
Another naked morning radiates
Another orange daybreak

This present will be different
I will press my hands together and be silent
Open my eyes when they're closed
Walk in the shadow of the stars
Stay awake when I'm sleeping
Today will be nothing like yesterday
I will hold myself still when they try to move me
Dress in fine silks
And blow kisses to strangers
Some of them are angels
Watching me face the mountain of ideas
Laughing at my indecision
While I'm trying to be someone else   »

If you are lucky
You will hear parts of your life played out on
A golden harp
The notes outline your shadow
Even when you dance without sound
Today will be a different day
I will cast my soul to the ageless
Listen to the music I heard as a child
I will feel like there is nothing to lose
Nothing to gain and
Everything to be alive for
If you're lucky
You will
Have a present like this
Wrapped as a gift
Given to you like the sunrise
Brighter than full moonlight

If you see it
You will call it Wabi Sabi
If you touch it
You would name it water
If you believe
You don't call it a thing

Lemn Sissay

rain

w	f	t	n	w	t	r	w	r	i	c
h	a	c		r			e			u
e	l	a	h		a			a	t	
n	l	h		i		t			's	n
t	l	e	e		i		h	i		
h	k	s		u		i	n	t		i
	s		n	m	n	n	b			a
e	t	t		p		k			h	n
r	h	o	e	t	h	f		o	e	
	e	f	h	a		o				
a		m	r	n	a		w			
i	y		b	e			f		m	w
		a	u		t	l		s	a	
n			t			l				a
					s				n	y

* Rain was commissioned in 2002 by Manchester City Council and appears as a mural on a very big wall in Manchester's Oxford Road.

Lemn Sissay

Perfect

You are so perfect
When you kick them, the leaves flit back to the trees
Look back to you and applaud
You are so perfect
Trees part in forests to share sun's shine
Squirrels watch you between acorns
Foxes wake

You are so perfect
Your winter coat buttons itself and hugs your heart
Library books unfurl on tables, stretch
And wait for you to walk past
Fast winter wind daren't touch you
But can't help brush your hair

You are so perfect
Rivers have built their own bridges
Knowing that one day you'll walk across them
Just to catch your reflection they left a pile of stones for you to throw
And the waves carry each stone to the bed, count them
look up at you and applaud

You are so perfect
Traffic lights time themselves days before you arrive
So your stride won't be broken and the cars can rest
And the world can stop
Tables in the city restaurants lay themselves to the waiter's amazement
Knowing that a man will stop for a coffee
Knowing that you will walk past at 3.30pm
And he'd been waiting for you all of his life too

Lemn Sissay

Applecart Art

Upset the art, smash the applecart
Sell it for firewood to warm hearts
Don't join the loop, the loop troupe
Don't hump through their hoops
Get stuck on sticky peaks of double speak
I'm clocking the click of the clique
I swim with the shallow
If they demand I be deep
Though I can hold my breath
Deeper than sleep, deeper than death

Upset the art, crash the Snapple cart
Sell it for cash and a brand new start
Turn cartwheels on the art wheels
If that's how your heart feels
To those who demand you stand by their pandect
Call them all cheats on call and collect
They're gargoyles hunched on their haunches
Stalking the walk at lunches and launches
They back bite back slap salubriously clap
With cleaver hands to stick in the back

Upset the art, trash the cattlecart
Start the stampede in the heart of the art
Don't play poker with the mediocre
Token filled pack full of jokers
The Class A offenders are pretenders
Protecting their pretence, return them to sender   »

Feel fierce flocks of fight and flowing
Know you're only as good as your last poem
Cut yourself, it should be ink you're bleeding
You're only as good as your last reading
Let wisdom be the weight of your wealth
And let your greatest competitor be yourself

Cherry Smyth

The Goddess of Love Must Still Do the Dishes

The love I had felt ordinary,
familiar as leather gloves can,
when they take on the shape of
the fingers and the back of the hand.
So I left it for something divine,
exciting as a strapless dress,
that miraculously stays up,
like tulips emerging from a vase.
But I felt too exposed, too mortal,
the competition in glitter was scary,
my hands seemed big and bare,
and I longed for something – well – ordinary.
Then a soothsayer told me to entwine
the divine with the ordinary,
the ordinary with the divine
and all would be hunky-dory,
in love,
with sensible gloves and fabulous dresses.

Cherry Smyth

Tunes for Baby

Each morning before you go to work, you dance.
Bobby Womack, Al Green, Barbara Mason.
You follow your hips, clip-clopping your tongue,
happy in the space your girlfriend leaves.
You send me anthologies of songs
to seduce, flatter, reconcile.
I play them, cooking or driving in traffic,
but only when removing make-up one night
do I hear the words:
He let you get away, baby...
When you move, you lose.
Your bragging via Barry White
makes me grin, even though, in your arms,
I don't feel found or lost and that's novel.
There's room to be absent, to float,
untranslated into sound;
two people with the same sweet tune
running through their heads.

II
Your steps are crafty, reassuring two women at once.
You need years of lovers behind you.
Nina Simone, Rickie Lee Jones, Stevie Wonder.
The Eagles were a surprise. *Lying Eyes*
is a cold wind, a young girl who thought
she was a foxy lady at seventeen,
the age my child could be now,
had I not stepped on the ferry,
the train, the bus to Streatham.   »

City girls just seem to find out early,
How to open doors with just a smile.
The scan monitor wasn't turned away
as though I'd welcome a black and white memory
of my whelk about to be washed up.
The gown was too short, too narrow
and I had to wear a paper cap,
as if long hair had done me wrong.
I could've died laughing.
Out the next day, not feeling any lighter,
jiggling on the bus, nipples dribbling.
I went straight back to school,
to Lloyd George and Pitt and Five Year Reforms,
a bag of books over my tummy, eyes down.

III
You've made love work over a decade
and I watch and listen and learn and then,
like crossing the road for the first time, alone,
toes to the curb, I'll take that single, convinced step.

Neil Sparkes
while the city sleeps

on those nights
when the city is wet
and gleaming
we steal our time
discovering there's more
inside a day
than last night
had expected to find
a certain monday
when the city is wet
and gleaming
this endless night
concrete notes
fall from the
tops of towers
your lips open
the earth opens
swallows me whole
a perfect stranger
    biting the silver
    rings in your ears
on those nights
when the city trembles
and tumbles around us
kissing the rain
from your face
fresh and beautiful
as new pictures and poems

Neil Sparkes

this is a reality

not the smiling face
but the rip in the stockings
of this beautiful girl

not raven hair waving
in a storm cloud
but the rain on her face

it's not the staggering
at the bar
but the drink that was drunk

not inventories
of crying lovers
but the glance
        of some new stranger

not walls sprayed
with rhyming graffiti
but a house brick

not the worn out wrists
in bedrooms
but the wartime of loving

it's not searching for truth
through denial
but what was actually said

Pauline Stewart

Sometimish Sea

Sometimes the sea is
calm as can be
waves rippling, glittering, peacefully,
sometimes though too
sea seems three shades of blue...
pick it up, hold it near
now sea falls free glistening clear
free
as   sand
liquid salt between
the   hands
Sometimish, stunning, sparkling sea
to and fro quite gracefully –
but if a hurricane should blow
sometimes sea gets cross you know...
no more blue slipping quietly by
but heavy leaden,
sea green / grey broody, electric
like stormy sky
sometimish mountainous sea
crashing down scarily,
raging, wrecking and drowning
hurling, whirling, smashing, scowling,
the sea batters and whips along
whistling winds
no singing songs
in its Wake
then calm
changes back into a friend
Sometimish Sea
Sometimish Sea
pure inconsistentsea...

SuAndi

DJstageone

This sound
Is silence
Without anything
Holding onto nothing
Is
This sound

This sound
Is the noise of life
The volume turned high by stress
Is
This sound

This sound

This sound
Is the smack of the baton
The bang of the gun
The scream of agony
The whimper of death
Is
This sound
This
Sound

But this sound
Is the warmth of love
The laying of this body
On this body   »

The uhmm
Of thighs entwined
That is this sound
Make
This sound
Make
This sound

Make this the sound of a
Revolution
Roaring
360 degree
Spinning spinning
And the rhythm rises
As the DJ controls
This sound
This sound
This
Sound

With its soulful chords
And beats that meets the heart in
One sound
This is the sound
This is the sound
This is   the sound
That moves
That wipes away misery
That is
The sound

And we need
This sound
Long live
DJ

SuAndi

Leaning Against Time

I see myself waiting
on this street corner of all that is England
Like a prostitute tired of the business
Yet waiting still
for that special lover.

Blind –
to the big pockets of small change
and no paper for creativity –
fat wallets with no lips to shape a conversation

My eyes turned down to the dirt of my situation
and see there reflected
the passing in all shades
of this
Black and white reality.

Those too lean to lay a hip next to
Those stomach-wider than desire
could stretch a leg over

I hear their mutterings
the cursing of
"who she think she is"
"too ugly for my taste"
"too worn"
"too wide"
"too choosy for her own good"   »

I hear
but like a deaf mute,
I remain as still as any public art commission
a subject of debate for some possibly,
possibly a waste of space,
life, for others
and therefore of absolutely no interest

On bad days
when chills whip past
this place I have taken for my own
I tell myself
this waiting will be the death of me
And the full glow of my living
will simply fade into that
darker shade of blood red dead

Sometimes I shuffle impatient
trying to hustle up an early arrival
but my welcoming dance
is mauled by the stubbornness of my leg(s)

My body takes on the bruising
of this waiting
as I am jostled by incidents out of my control
But I remain steadfast
And if you pass by
you will see me
A sentinel
Leaning Against Time

Steve Tasane
Dream State

So I'm a revolutionary poet in mediaeval Paris policed by Big Brother jobsworths who hate long hair, funky music and boys wearing pink. Instead of sniffer dogs they have pubic hair-covered pot-bellied pigs desperate to snuffle up hash truffles then float off on their backs off their heads down the Seine.

Anybody not wanting to be nobody meets in a coffee shop on Hooplah Hill, managed by Madam Fandango. Sample menu: brandy chai, garlic fry-up, Absinthe, chilli ice cream and the juice of freshly squeezed sonnets.

Madam Fandango insists we hang our hang-ups at the door. Bags of mismatched screws, mouldy pipes and buckled wheels. At the end of each day, she crushes them into tight little balls and eats them raw. But she dishes up sweet, life-enhancing soup, and introduced me to Aphrodite Wah-Wah. Everybody has an angel. Aphrodite Wah-Wah is mine.

Concepts float like fresh blossom round the grey girders of Gridlock Square. But thick-set roadblocks stop and search t-shirts for unlicensed imagination, and stamp them. Aphrodite and I tongue-twist past, kissing the sky, floating on clouds of love-rumpled bedding.

We look down and see Big Brother's Big Daddy with his escape-proof hand-knit cardie at the ready and an Old Lady with tea on the go. "This'll bring you down, this'll bring you down," they hiss, grinning, chucking the cups up at us. "Would you like another?" Bam-Bam, their pet pot-bellied pig, snorkels up a bucketful of Tetley's tastiest. Big Daddy nuzzles behind her ears. His dentures are in because he's about to make a press statement. He's a smiling, lying crocodile at a back garden barbecue.

The little speech he makes is guaranteed to bring us down. We crash-land slap-bang in the middle of Monday Morning Rat Run, where Gridlock Square is dry-retching glass-eyed Yes-Men.

Big Daddy's caressing his belly and telling us to follow the fine example. "Follow the fine example – you'll come out good." He pats a rush hour of backs, hassling Donutheads into open-plan confinement. The day drizzles in disappointment.

Aphrodite Wah-Wah isn't her real name. The name on her Blockbusters membership slip is two question marks kissing in the middle, booffing their heads. I said, "How do you pronounce that?" She shrugged and licked my frontal lobe. Aphrodite Wah-Wah just struck. It was love at first sight, and she calls me all the names under the sun.

So Aphrodite says, "Quick let's slip by on a song and a dance," and just as Big Daddy's declaring marital law we're hoofing it up Hooplah Hill for a hoedown at Madam Fandango's. We've been working on a new poetic form – a Tai Chi interpretation of toilet graffiti set in the metre of pigeonsong.

But when we get to the top of the hill, Madam Fandango's is boarded up. Terminator 3 is posted outside, with an I've been left in charge lilt to his jaw.

He spots us and asks if we're warm enough. He tries to give us a hand-knit cardie, and make us drink tea. He clearly means business, so we leg it, flapping as hard as we can. We take off, leaving Arnie-Man tutting and shaking his dishcloth.

Madam Fandango is in danger. Her name tops the official list of banned substances. Big Daddy has issued a vivisection order. He wants to pick her apart, isolate and splice whichever gene generates her genius, and stick it in a jam jar at the back of the pantry next to well-past-its-use-by-date baking powder.

We need a plan. Head back to earth. As Aphrodite Wah-Wah hides round the corner, I walk back to Arnie-Man and drink his tea. I put on that hand-knit straitjacket. I eat the chocolate digestive. I'm going home.

The front door shudders behind us. "Right, my lad," Big Daddy grunts, giving me a pudding-bowl haircut and a medicinal compound of mustard and marmite. He takes my fingerprints, and though the flesh of my fingers bleeds raw, I'm given a Brillo pad with which to scrub my dirty bits. I'm planted in a giant pot in the corner next to the telly and nailed to the wall so I don't lean too much into the sun. The telly taunts me, singing Kum Ba Yah Ma Lord Kum Ba Yah while Big Daddy waffles on about Big Daddies and reminisces about when Bam-Bam was just a piglet and he invites all the other Big Daddies to come round and piss in my pot. The Old Lady sticks a tube down me to ensure a continuous supply of Tetleys, all to a soundtrack of Kum Ba Yah Ma Lord Kum Ba Yah.

Big Daddy has his knees spread, sitting in his Big Daddy armchair, stroking his Big Daddy belly, eyeing me up and muttering, "Ooh, you'll come out good, you will, you'll come out good." Madam Fandango is whimpering behind the sofa. The doorbell rings. "Get that, will yer."

Is that him, or is it me?

"I said get that, will yer."

It's me! Ohh, I look down and I'm wearing slippers. I've got a gut that's as good as it's gonna get, but best of all, everywhere I look I see me. The Old Lady asks if I'd like some toast, and I go, "Aye, go on then." Then she asks me if I'd like some Jaffa Cakes, and I go "Aye, go on then." And as she goes to answer the door, she asks me if I'd like some more tea.

And as she goes I look round and it's him and me, Big Daddy. I like what I see. I look him in the eye. I grab him by the ears and I give him a kiss. I never kissed Big Daddy before. Our tongues collide like a car crash of lies. I suck up all his deception. I gulp his guts straight down. I eat the heart, though it's dry and hard. It's quite tasty though, so I guzzle down a few other bits. I chuck the skin and bones to my pot-bellied pet.

Old Lady comes back in, and behind her is Aphrodite Wah-Wah. Thing is, all she does is touch my hand, and I'm me again. Full of sunshine. So we untie Madam Fandango while Bam-Bam hoovers up the last few crumbs, and we step out.

I'm a revolutionary poet in mediaeval Paris. I like it here. Think I'm gonna stay.

Steve Tasane
Thugbaby

She's an ocean of poison and I've got to swim it
She's a roughneck sadist having her break
She's the cat-eyed road – I'm over the limit
She's the piled-up cost of one mistake
Thugbaby – she makes me ache

She's one mean mother and I'm illegitimate
She's a smile that feasts on human blood
She's a surgical probe that's just getting intimate
She's the Good Samaritan up to no good
Thugbaby – makes my heart thud

She's a mattress mottled with amazing stains
She's the aching ribs of a snake embrace
She's 24-carat ankle chains
She's a rainbow bruise on my raging face
Thugbaby – a disgrace

She's a sleeping lioness just getting peckish
She's red hot chilli on a groping hand
She's a perfect dish left out to perish
She's pesticide in Disneyland
Thugbaby – on remand

She's a booby-trapped war zone – I'm the squaddie
She's a million maggots and I'm her meat
She's a virus clinging to my antibody
She's sexual illness and I'm her gleet
Thugbaby – she's on heat   »

She's a slow learner – I'm her afterthought
She's a lo-cost barcode on my skin
Her heart's on holiday – I'm her last resort
She's way out when I need to stay in
Thugbaby – original sin

Greg Tate
The End of Summer

The world will go boom when all the Big Trucks ghost. No longer will an utterly dramatic suicide letter arrive from Palm Springs and drive us to distraction. No longer will you go run and tell one of the Big Trucks how you told the butch to stop calling your house but she just wouldn't listen.

No longer will one of the Big Trucks take your hand and pet your fur and comfort your mind with the news that, "A headless blonde with hairy armpits is all she is to you now."

Hosing down Harlem's streets of love, the Big Trucks of this world used to go boom and make everything all right. But soon all the Big Trucks will ghost and we'll be left to our own explosive devices, be left to indelicately settle our own incendiary scores.

The last lunch Marlena and I will have before the clandestine phase of The Wars ends will be in L'Aviatrix, her favorite bistro. The meal will consist of boiled calamari and arugula goat cheese portobello mushroom salad. Those familiar Negro delicacies. This will be the day Marlena will tell me how she believes she can fly because she has dreamt of wings and webbing which run from her torso to her armpits. (This will also be the day she shows up to lunch high on Race-Memory and starts babbling about Black Bolt and the Inhumans and the Fantastic Four.)

This too will be the day Marlena insists she has been flying without wings for at least a week. She will recall, "and with pinpoint accuracy," sez she, shooting down whole battalions of the White Bodypolitic while bleeding profusely from a gunshot wound to the head while tumbling out of a three-story window. Scuttling to her feet she vanishes like smoke before the local constabulary arrived. Sez she.

Near-death, she will conspiratorially whisper, is just like an arpeggio: a rippling moment of total clarity where every single event of one's life rings out its hidden lyrical truths and sub-harmonic buried treasures.

Near-death Marlena also claims to have had an epiphany about me. The epiphany being that unlike Romeo or herself, I would never die simply because I was not a Man but a symbol.

"Your symbolic virtues alone will keep you going long after me and everyone else in our humble little group of assassins has been sent to their happy hunting grounds."

"Your immortality, Pruitt," she informs me between several bouts of narcoleptic collapse, "has been guaranteed by God. Your going on and on and on after the rest of us have crashed and burned will be no accident. It has always been your destiny."

Not to be boastful, but she wasn't telling me anything I didn't already know. I had long known that no matter how much I loved my Big Trucks, my Romeos and my Marlenas and even my Cals, I could not make them immortals.

At best I could only make them historic, legendary, mythical. I was doomed to a long life, to perpetual revolution.

I was everything my parents had ever designed me to be.

Upon expectoration from the womb, I got sent flying on a snowblind course rife with river runs, Checkpoint Charlies, wailing walls, slaveship diagrams, nigga revenge scenarios and will-to-Black Power fantasies. Free will was nowhere to be found as I got sent flying towards my inbred objective: the Black Quanta.

Something would die in me months after that lunch when I indeed found a winged Marlena broken and mashed on the pavement, blood drooling from all manner of torn tissue and novel orifices. All over her body, her moist and tender skin had been violently scraped open.

Abrasions everywhere were hydraulically pumping out tissue, blood, pus. Whatever broke in me however was not my desire to make war on the White Bodypolitic and serve the Black Quanta.

Later still, right before she died in my arms, I told her, "You always were a real cut-up, dollface." I said this not to be cruel but because she loved the cruel-acting side of me. The snide remark side. The side responsible for my gallows humor at the operating table and my bedside manner of a coroner and cadaverists. So unlike my one and only true love Dark Jane, who loved me for nothing more than my stupid fits and spells of rhyming like Simple Simon / Bono Pruitt the pieman. That side came with my pussy hound with white noise for brains side and my me and the boys psychotropically intoxicated and clueless-in-Gaza, bombed-out-our-minds side. All the parts of me which were angst-free and oblivious to all clear and present dangers and which made me so unlike Marlena's man Romeo, who was forever going on about midnight suns and mushroom clouds over Harlem.

Therein lies the major difference between me and our man Rome.

I never talked revolution.

I just made it happen.

Quietly, efficiently, masterfully. Bono the stealth bomber versus Romeo the publicity hound. What a team we made. Poor Romeo couldn't just walk the walk. And having to talk the talk would prove to be not his, but Harlem's undoing.

Poor Romeo never dreamed his beloved Marlena's life would end before his own. That hers would end before the Big Trucks stopped hosing down Harlem's streets of love. He also never forgave me for revealing how tantalized I was by the sight of her dying form or admitting how much love she and I had made before she wilted, folded, spindled and mutilated in my tender embrace. (There at the end of our long march, she and I were just a step away from becoming necrophiliacs. Like so many, we had begun our rebel lives as free radicals married to the cause and had ended them as a species of polymorphous perverse. It was irony hardly lost on such long-standing deathmongers as ourselves.)

Then again, we had not invented our revolution, we only inherited it. It had been willed to us by the one, the only, Camelot Drexel.

The same Drexel who had invented Race-Memory and in so doing resuscitated the purple promise of America for all its big-lipped stranglers and drive-by shooters. Hosing down Harlem's streets of love, Drexel had given sudden and addictive hope (or do I mean dope?) to more hapless murderers than a few, each of whose necks were strung with brash pendants advertising their Neanderthal descent from the likes of the James and Barker boys.

Success had strangely made Drexel, no uptown boy himself, quite intimate with their type of fatalist: the type who keep the smell of nooses under their breaths. As their liberator, he'd cheered them on as those invisible ropes had dissolved from round their necks. As their liberator, he'd applauded as the waxen twists of strawcord had fallen and dripped down past their waists to tickle the brand new johnsons he'd installed onto their groins along the way to spiraling about the drainage holes on the cutting-room floor.

The problem with Drexel's notion of Black male freedom was that Drexel had gone too far. In so doing, he'd reduced the race's bone-hard numbers to the few, the proud, the soft, cuddly-freaky and habit-forming. All of which left Romeo and me the task of renewing our peoples' warrior ranks. A task for which we were ill-equipped, though properly amped. Though we were both only five and six years of age at the time and hardly aware of being destined to raze Harlem in the name of genetically terrorizing the White Bodypolitic, we went at the thing, our mission, with gusto, from grades K-12 and beyond.

Firebombs over Harlem and bloodbaths aside, this is a love story. Take a whole heap of terrorism out of the picture and what you've got is just your average All-African-American Love Story. The only difference between this love story and other romances you might have entertained is that, by the time you read this, the lovers in question will have become dust bunnies.

Fit and proper subjects of that branch of particle physics for which whisk brooms and vacuum cleaners were invented.

These particular quantum black bucktoothed rodents, Romeo Void and Marlena Plane, had not started out in life obsessed with race revolt and bondage and angry ancestors ghosts. Unlike me they had to be reprogrammed first. Even though their forebears had been byproducts of a genetic experiment gone awry, The Making of the American Nigga, by any other name, they, like so many before them, had not come into this world full of bile and rage at the White Bodypolitic for trespasses against their phenotype and genotype: all those branded and reviled name-brand spooks the country still had not made up its mind about after looking at them squirm for six generations. As in that oft-repeated question of antebellum debate, "But what is to be done about The Niggers?" What is to be done about all those ill-fated but sure-footed creatures spat and shat out by the New World who somehow managed to keep on a-steppin'? (Focus the lens and crippled buckdancers can be seen as eternally plaintive silhouettes. Titanic wounded ships who refuse to completely sink beneath the horizon as long as there is one more sad, buck and wing song to sing.)

These lovers we speak of were not born aflame but quickly caught afire and just as quickly became flickers, fading embers, then finally just another damned beautiful pile of mythic ashes swept into yesterday's news.

There is a war the damned and the beautiful will forever wage against the fast-spreading virus of human boredom. A war the damned and the beautiful will always lose only to sustain the worst injury of all: that slow, excruciating fall from grace which accompanies all flashes-in-the-pan into never-never-land. So here lies a forgotten Black prince and his faded yella princess, high-flying eminences in their time but now only quaint obscure curiosities, non-beings of a peculiar pedigree and historical distinction. In their full bloom, they were ornate and ostentatious creatures, outspoken about their purchases and their politics and possibly the most flagrant idolators of themselves the world had ever known. They were also too cute to be believed. So cute you might have killed them if they hadn't been such adept killers of killers themselves. Romeo Void and Marlena Plane: two marvelous spinning tops now fixed in mirror-orbit around each other's dead star-turns. The sort of couple who remind themselves daily of their own magnificence by dotting and freckling every available inch of their home with Him and Her portraits of themselves partying hard, politicking harder, inflicting pain harder still, all the while tossing seriously sexy-eyed looks at the camera. (A bouyant tableau of unrepentant narcissism adorned their walls, the best chronicle we have of one lost tribe's zest for living, dying, laughing and running Harlem literally, figuratively, despotically.)

Harlem had made them famous and so Harlem keeps their legend alive. Enshrining and ennobling the couple's memory with that selective amnesia typical of oppressed and icon-starved peoples everywhere. If we wish to solve the mystery of their swift rise, fall and erasure, it is to Harlem we must return. Theirs was a great American love story, even if one more tragic than the rest in the end because they didn't just up and die as they should have when their revolution failed. No, all dressed up in militant regalia when there really was nowhere for them to go but down, down, down to sleep beneath the graveyard dirt, they rose from the ashes and started doing the funky chicken.

Settling, in other words, for the more common trope: an afterlife of self-parody. Two clown figures of the new minstrel circuit withering and dithering on the vine in the name of their spent days of insurrection.

Thom the World Poet

Black Hole Fears

stumble sideways saints
beggars via roadsides
sides of demi-gods on plates
like heads of lonely dancers
she works for tips in bars
smoking ban teetotals
tottering into unemployment
she picks up less in bars
goes silent as a submariner
tattoos her insides/blue ink poems
scratched scorched stories
she wins awards for masochism
"the lonely life of writers"
"how to suffer for no reason"
"epic sagas cut by pens"
her hits are drug-addicted
her scores are SlamFinals
she is Armageddon judgments
she is professionally silent
published on the Internet
all her friends adore her
she has hidden habits which attract
the lonely to her webcamera
she will be rich next year
her new career in cinema

Leah Thorn
excerpt from *Watch*

in memory of Manny Thorn

*Be strong in the honour of your father and do not leave him all the
days of your life. Even if he loses sense, let him do all that he wishes
and do not shame him all the days of his life*

– Ben Sira [3:12-13]

I am the keeper
of my father's memory
I have learnt him
by heart   I steal
enduring power of attorney
of his words, gather fractures
as he forgets
what he has forgotten

once
he was my magician
now frantic
I perform tricks
to magic him
back

blue feelings
for a father who suits blue,
blue suit
flecks in tweeds and smooth
to touch,   my father
with blue streaks in his grey eyes

I am the tailor's daughter who cannot find the thread
I am to bind my parents   overlock them together   but my
needles break   threads break   stitches skip   stitches loop
material puckers   I check upper tension is not too tight

        my father jungle-hacks through jumbled thoughts
        wills me in   and at moments of connection,
        eyes wet, he smiles
        squeezes my hand
        I imprint his jangles into my brain
        magpie his phrases to savour him   later

the flat stole your gold watch
snaps your threads
bruises you
doors fuse
flat is on the move
out to confuse you
WHO IS DOING THIS
to you   you want to live
           elsewhere
you tell me   *we're lost here   living so far from ourselves*

alzheimer's orlando transmutes gender and number them
to we he to she he she to I the Her your people never you you

memory-soaked skin
cries in the night
tongue untied
my father's scream
a razor blade of raw rage
                        awake
tattooed with nighttime
punishment, coiling snakes
of blood roughly etched
by those too tired,
too enraged
to notice

    at the point of falling back into water
    at the moment before breaking the surface
    at the moment of off-balance and flying
    at that moment arms flay like backwards backstroke
    and I call out to god, god

I am scared of water closing over my head
my father is water, sweeping me away
imperfect water floods my father's brain   my father is water
he spits in my face   burns me with his spittle
fills my eyes with water
not all water has perfect memory

        remember by recital   by ritual
        remember zakhar   a sacred command
        remember one hundred and sixty nine times
        remember talmudic dictum
        remember ache in commemoration
        remember the secret of relief
                              is remembrance

Christopher Twigg
A Vision

The sardine can I see so very clear
the flaky sardines in their golden oil
like corpses all dishevelled flaking foil
packed in as close as travellers so near
shoulder to shoulder on the underground
on fetid summer evenings turning home
no more like sharp adventurers to roam
in darksome waters where their friends are found
Their friendship now is tightness new defined
no breathing space, decapitated, tails
confined and sheltered finally in-sealed
and if to wiggle they were once inclined
now steep compression energy derails
until on opening day they are revealed.

Christopher Twigg

A Ripple

A ripple on its journey to the grave
came riding through the room where silence held
sway – as in forests after trees are felled –
the air itself was like a water wave
where minnows flickered clouds of silver swelled

Curtis Walker
Maggie T

I was sixteen years old when I first performed poetry for Apples & Snakes. Curtis and Ishmael was the name of our double act – young, black and sexy was the way we wanted to be thought of but young, black and angry was the way we were described. I'm still working on the sexy thing.

The first poem I wrote was called **Maggie T***. This was a poem dedicated to Margaret Thatcher, in a time of great civil unrest. Miners' strike, mass unemployment and* **Tucker's Luck**, *the Todd Carty spin-off from* **Grange Hill** *was about to be axed.*

Yes, it was a time for social commentary. Ishmael and I were ready to join Billy Bragg and others to fight the fight, armed not with a knife or gun, but with a Bic pen and lots of Tippex.

Maggie T, Maggie T
What you doing fi we
We are a part of your community
but still you a tek advantage of we
Maggie T, Maggie T
What you doing fi we

I notice last week se police force
Get new uniform and new riot shield
New helmet and new truncheon
This week me hear se dem a go start carry gun
But wait
What good is that to me?
I don't want to become no damn PC   »

Maggie T, Maggie T
What you doing fi we
We are a part of your community
but still you a tek advantage of we
Maggie T, Maggie T
What you doing fi we

Feel the power...

It went on and on but that's all I can remember, honest. Apples & Snakes,
Curtis Walker salutes you.

Claire Williamson

If I Could

If I could write a poem which
changes key in exactly the right
places, like your favourite songs...

If I could write a poem which
switches from major to minor, tossing a pebble in
your rib cage...

If I could write a poem which
turns heads as it walks
down the street...

If I could write a poem
which smiles when you fix
your eyes on it...

If I could write a poem which
plays drinking games with
you when you are lonely...

If I could...
I would write a poem for you.

Ann Ziety

Before and After Wediflop

Before Wediflop
Luvy dovy
Sugar bunny
Canoodles cuddles oodles doodles
Yummy lips go kissy kissy
Hands entwine in total blissy
Much feely nice nice
Together in paradise

Edible dwarling sweetiepops
Pumpkin dumpling chuckiechops
You are my ecclescake
I am your squirrelkins
Squeegie ickle sunny buttocks
Scintillating smackeroos
Together we're a superdooper
Pair of smashing snookumses
Let's tie a soppy knot of blissful
Kissful snoggy wediflop
So the yippee yippee yum yum
Just won't stop

After Wediflop
Big pile of filthy festering frantic
Growling
Howling
Washing-up in sink

"I'm not doing it"
"I'm not doing it either, fat git"

Ann Ziety

Yucca Tree

My yucca didn't looka bit
Like a yucca ought to looka
Which is probably because
The fucka was a spider plant

Artist biographies

Chris Abani
Award-winning poet and novelist Chris Abani's new novel, *Graceland*, will be published by Farrar, Straus & Giroux in February 2004. His latest collection of poetry is *Daphne's Lot* (Red Hen Press, 2003). He is a Middleton Fellow at the University of Southern California and teaches in the MFA Program at Antioch University, Los Angeles and the University of California, Riverside.

Dannie Abse
Dannie Abse's poetry collections include *Selected Poems*, winner of a Welsh Arts Council Literature Award; *Pythagoras*; *Way Out in the Centre*; *Ask the Bloody Horse*; and *White Coat, Purple Coat: Collected Poems 1948–1988*. His published fiction includes *Ash on a Young Man's Sleeve* and *O Jones, O Jones*. He has edited many poetry anthologies. *Goodbye, Twentieth Century: An Autobiography* includes and updates his first volume of autobiography, *A Poet in the Family*. His most recent novel is *The Strange Case of Dr Simmonds & Dr Glass* and *The Two Roads Taken: A Prose Miscellany* has just been published.

Shanta Acharya
Born in Orissa, India, Shanta Acharya has lived in London since 1985. Her doctoral study, *The Influence of Indian Thought on Ralph Waldo Emerson*, was published by The Edwin Mellen Press in 2001. Her two books of poetry are *Numbering Our Days' Illusions* (Rockingham Press, 1995) and *Not This, Not That* (Rupa & Co, India, 1994). Her collection, *Looking In, Looking Out*, is due in 2004.

Adisa
Adisa's debut in performance poetry won Apples & Snakes' Best New Performance Poet award in 1994. He has since performed to a wide variety of audiences in venues from pubs to universities to the Hackney Empire.

John Agard
Playwright, poet, short-story and children's writer John Agard was born in Guyana. In 1993 he was appointed Writer in Residence at the South Bank Centre and became Poet in Residence at the BBC. He won the Paul Hamlyn Award for Poetry in 1997. His published poetry includes *Man to Pan* (1982), winner of the Casa de las Américas Prize, *Limbo Dancer in Dark Glasses* (1983), *Mangoes and Bullets: Selected and New Poems 1972–84* (1985) and *Weblines* (2000).

Patience Agbabi

Patience Agbabi has published two collections of poetry, *Transformatrix* and *R.A.W.*, which won the Excelle Literary Award for Poetry. She has performed worldwide and run courses for the Arvon Foundation and the British Council and was resident poet at the Poetry Society and a London-based tattoo parlour. She is currently an Associate Lecturer in Creative Writing at Cardiff University and working on her third book, *Body Language*.

Jamika Ajalon

American-born Jamika Ajalon has performed at venues worldwide, with the Urban Poets, the Tony Allen Band and the Shrine. She often tours France with dub group *Zenzile* and is included on the albums *Zenzile Meets Jamika 5+1, Sound Patrol* and *Totem*, as well as Eva Gardner's compilation *aphrodisia 3*. She has been published in many collections including *Bittersweet, Gargoyle, modern love* and *Kin*.

Sara-Jane Arbury

Sara-Jane Arbury was a finalist in the first UK All-Comers Poetry Slam in 1985, and has since performed her poetry on TV, radio and at racecourses; at arts centres, clubs and festivals; in restaurants, schools and shopping malls. She has held writing residencies in Bristol, Camelford, Dublin and four Oxfordshire village shops. She co-hosts poetry slams around the country and is the Director of the Voices Off programme at Cheltenham Festival of Literature. In 1995, she co-founded Pimp$ of the Alphab£t, which staged the *Truth Is Optional* tour.

Steve Aylett

Steve Aylett was born in Bromley at the end of the Sixties. His first book, *The Crime Studio*, was generally regarded as a cry for help. *Bigot Hall, Slaughtermatic, The Inflatable Volunteer, Toxicology, Only an Alligator, Atom, The Velocity Gospel, Dummyland, Karloff's Circus* and *Shamanspace* followed. Published by Orion (UK) and Four Walls Eight Windows (US), Aylett was a finalist for the 1998 Philip K Dick Award. His books and stories have been translated into Spanish, Czech, Italian, French, Japanese, German, Russian and Greek.

Shamim Azad

Storyteller and poet Shamim Azad has compiled and produced anthologies in Bengali and English, developed oral histories and prepared intergenerational projects for publication. She also runs INSETs on Parent and Family Education. Shamim's work in English is published in several anthologies. Her publications in Bengali include collections of poems, short stories and a novel.

Francesca Beard

Francesca Beard was born in Kuala Lumpur and grew up in Penang. She has performed for the British Council in Azerbaijan, Bulgaria and Columbia and gone bravely into schools all round Britain. Her work features in many anthologies and her chapbook, *Cheap*, is now in its fourth imprint. Her first one-woman show, *Chinese Whispers*, enjoys a three-week run at BAC, London, in November 2003, commissioned and developed by Apples & Snakes and BAC.

Beyonder

Beyonder is a two-time Urban Griots poetry slam champion who has performed all over Europe, at the Nuyorican Café in New York and the De Nachten Festival in Amsterdam and Antwerp. He is published in the *Loungin'* anthology and has a CD out entitled *Just Be*.

Paul Birtill

Paul Birtill was born in Liverpool in 1960 and moved to London in his early twenties. One of his plays was short-listed for the Verity Bargate Award. *So Far So Bad* is Birtill's second collection of poems, dealing with his favourite themes of death, relationships and mental illness with his usual brand of dark humour and deep-veined irony.

Valerie Bloom

Valerie Bloom was born in Clarendon, Jamaica and came to England in 1979. She has run writing courses for the Arvon Foundation, had residencies in England, Ireland, Northern Ireland and Wales, and performed widely in Britain and the Caribbean. She has published several books for children and her poems have been included in over 200 anthologies, in the GCSE exam syllabi in England and Wales, in the CXC syllabus in the Caribbean, in the *Poems on the Underground* series and as *the Independent's* Poem of the Day.

Jean 'Binta' Breeze

Jean 'Binta' Breeze came through on the rhythms and reverberations of reggae and was first known as a dub poet. As an actress, dancer, choreographer and theatrical director, Jean has performed her work worldwide, including tours of the US, Europe, South East Asia, Africa and the Caribbean. She has published several books, written film and TV scripts, directed theatre productions, contributed to many records and been anthologised the world over.

Pete Brown

Pete Brown became a professional poet in 1960, working with *New Departures* and taking part in the famed Albert Hall poetry readings of 1965 and 1966. He wrote the lyrics for most of Cream's major hits, including *Sunshine of Your Love, White Room, I Feel Free* and *Politician*. Among many others, Pete has worked with BB King and Robert Plant sideman Innes Sibun. He wrote and produced Dick Heckstall-Smith's album *Blues and Beyond*.

Dana Bryant

New York jazz-poetry diva Dana Bryant came through on the Nuyorican spoken-word wave of the '90s, drawing on jazz and hip-hop and taking her inspiration from the work of Jayne Cortez and Ntozake Shange. She has performed all over the world and collaborated with some of the most innovative artists working today.

Ainsley Burrows

Ainsley Burrows produced a book of poetry, *Black Angels with Sky Blue Feathers* and an album of spoken word called *Cataclysm*. Since then, he has published a second volume of poetry, two CDs and has just completed his first novel.

Billy Childish

A cult figure in America, Europe and Japan, and one of the most prolific creative spirits of his generation, Billy Childish has published more than 30 collections of poetry, recorded 100+ full-length independent LPs and produced more than 2000 paintings over the past 25 years. Grounded in the punk ethic of '77, Childish's work is explosive and uncompromising, yet never loses its humour.

Lana Citron

London-based Dubliner Lana Citron is the author of three novels, *Transit*, *Spilt Milk* and *Sucker*. Other works include short stories and poetry published in various anthologies, stories *Now & Forever*, *Awakening Chamber* and *Missing Pink* broadcast on Radio 4, and her award-winning short film, *I Was the Cigarette Girl*.

John Cooper Clarke

John Cooper Clarke is one of pioneers of performance poetry, a punk poet who has travelled with the times and yet looks more or less exactly as he did twenty years ago, emerging even less marked by the ravages of a rock'n'roll lifestyle than Keith Richards. He adores vodka martinis, currently has two CDs out and is rather a shy chap, really.

Sally Pomme Clayton

Storyteller Sally Pomme Clayton has been performing for adults and children since 1984. She has performed at the British Museum, the Hay-on-Wye Festival, the South Bank Centre; in Alaska, Norway, Sweden and Portugal; and for the British Council in Spain, Kyrgyzstan and Kazakhstan. She has published several collections of stories and her next book, *Tales Told in Tents*, about Central Asia, is published by Frances Lincoln in 2004.

Samantha Coerbell

Samantha Coerbell has been active on the New York poetry scene since 1991, and has performed with numerous musicians and writers. A native New Yorker with Trinidadian roots, Samantha is currently working at Washington Square Arts, booking performance tours in the US and UK. She performed with Apples & Snakes in the Edinburgh Festival in 1998.

Merle Collins

Merle Collins was born in Grenada. Her first works were anthologised in *Callaloo: A Grenada Anthology*. Her first collection of poetry, *Because the Dawn Breaks*, was published a year later. In 1985, Collins joined *The African Dawn*. She has served as the Writer in Residence at the London Borough of Waltham Forest and worked as a freelance writer and lecturer. She published her first novel, *Angel*, in 1987 and her second, *The Colour of Forgetting*, in 1995.

Patric Cunnane

Patric Cunnane is a veteran on the performance poetry scene. His work has been published in numerous magazines and anthologies and broadcast on radio. He has run many successful workshops in South London. His latest collection, *Dance Music*, is now available.

Fred D'Aguiar

Fred D'Aguiar was born in London of Guyanese parentage. His most recent poetry collection is *An English Sampler: Selected Poems* and his latest novel is *Bethany Bettany*, both published by Chatto & Windus. He held various writing residences in the UK before moving to America to become an English professor at Virginia Tech, where he teaches creative writing.

Joolz Denby

Joolz Denby has been a professional writer and performer for over 20 years, and gives workshops and master classes in creative writing and performance skills in the UK and Germany. She has performed at 5 Edinburgh Festivals, 20 Glastonbury Festivals and at hundreds of venues worldwide. Her books of poetry and short stories include *Errors of the Spirit* and *The Pride of Lions*. Her first novel, *Stone Baby*, won the CWA New Crime Writer Award and was short-listed for the John Creasey Award 2000. Her second novel is *Corazon* (HarperCollins, 2001).

Denrele

Denrele is both a published and performance poet, as well as part of Malika's Poetry Kitchen collective. She has performed at many leading poetry venues.

Michael Donaghy

Michael Donaghy has won numerous awards for his elegant, passionate poetry. Oxford University Press published two of his collections: *Shibboleth*, which won the Whitbread Poetry Prize and the Geoffrey Faber Memorial Prize, and *Errata*, which was selected for the New Generation Poets promotion.

Claire Dowie

Claire Dowie has written and performed a variety of stand-up theatre plays, including A*dult Child/Dead Child* (1988 *Time Out* Theatre Award), *Why Is John Lennon Wearing a Skirt?* (1991 London Fringe Award), *Death and Dancing, Drag Act, Leaking from Every Orifice, All Over Lovely* and *Easy Access*. She has recently completed a new play and is working on her first novel, *Creating Chaos*.

Stella Duffy

Stella Duffy's novels, *Singling Out the Couples, Eating Cake* and *Immaculate Conceit*, are published by Sceptre; her crime novels are published by Serpent's Tail. Her latest novel is *State of Happiness* (Virago, 2004). She also writes short stories and feature articles, and for radio and theatre. She co-edited the anthology *Tart Noir* (Pan&Berkley) and won the CWA 2002 Short Story Dagger Award. She adapted *Immaculate Conceit* with the National Youth Theatre at the Lyric Hammersmith.

Helen East

Helen's publications include: *Dora the Storer, the Arthur's Aunt Preschool Series* (featured on BBC playtime, published by Simon & Schuster), *Two Tongue Tales* (Folktale Centre Publishing) and *Look Lively, Rest Easy* (A&C Black). She also writes for the BBC World Service.

Zena Edwards

Zena Edwards has toured the UK and Europe extensively. *Healing Pool* is her debut album of poetry, vocals and music. She has performed for Jonzi D's *Aeroplane Man* (percussion and vocals), on BBC Radio 4's *Poetry Please*, Guy Barker's *World Café* for BBC Radio 3, London Live Radio, and in various short films which won awards in festivals across Europe and America.

Lucy English

Born in Sri Lanka and raised in London, Lucy English performs regularly in Bristol and London and has appeared at many prestigious festivals. Lucy's work is featured in the anthologies *Oral* (Sceptre, 2000), *Gargoyle 42* and *Shortfuse*. She has three novels published by Fourth Estate, *Selfish People, Our Dancing Days* and *Children of Light* and is currently working on a fourth.

Amy Evans

Born in North Carolina, Amy Evans moved to Berlin after completing her studies, where she began devising and performing spoken word pieces, working actively within the Black German community. She earned her Masters degree at Goldsmiths College in 2001. Her first play, *Achidi J's Final Hours*, was awarded a Verity Bargate bursary from Soho Theatre in London in 2002. Amy is now based in Berlin where she writes, performs and teaches workshops at Humboldt University.

Bernardine Evaristo

Bernardine Evaristo's *The Emperor's Babe* was published by Penguin in 2001. Her novel-in-verse, *Lara*, won the EMMA Best Novel Award in 1999. She received an Arts Council Writer's Award in 2000, has completed 23 tours worldwide, held writing residencies in Zimbabwe, New York and Cape Town and is a Contributing Editor to *Wasafiri* literature journal.

Dele Fatunla

Dele Fatunla has been involved in the London poetry scene for five years, performing at the Greenwich Docklands International Festival and Apples & Snakes, among other venues. He is studying for a degree in African Studies and Politics.

Lawrence Ferlinghetti

A prominent voice of the wide-open poetry movement that began in the '50s, Lawrence Ferlinghetti writes poetry, fiction, theatre, art criticism, film narration and essays. He founded the legendary City Lights Bookstore in San Francisco and launched City Lights Publishers. In the '60s and '70s, Ferlinghetti's *A Coney Island of the Mind* was the most popular poetry book in the US, has since been translated into nine languages, and there are nearly 1,000,000 copies in print. His most recent books are *A Far Rockaway of the Heart* and *How to Paint Sunlight*.

Ruth Forman

An award-winning writer, Ruth Forman lives in Los Angeles. Her first book of poetry, *We Are the Young Magicians* (Beacon Press, 1993) won the prestigious Barnard New Women Poets Prize. Her second book, *Renaissance* (Beacon Press, 1998), won the 1999 Pen Oakland Josephine Miles Award for Poetry and received a nomination for the Pulitzer Prize. Her work is widely anthologised.

Julian Fox

As a child, Julian Fox wanted to be a pop star, an airline pilot and then an artist. He studied Fine Art at Norwich and started writing as a theatre stage door keeper, to while away an eight-hour shift. Julian began performing at various poetry evenings, and presented *A Slacker's Opera*, a collage of his songs, poems, drawings and dance routines, at the Edinburgh Festival in 2000. He is currently working on his fourth piece, *Spaces for New Role Models*.

Mat Fraser

Mat Fraser is an actor, writer, musician and sometime TV presenter. His recent written work includes his one-man show, *Sealboy: Freak*, which has toured nationally and abroad, and his international award-winning documentary film for Channel 4, *Born Freak*. Channel 4 has just aired his documentary on cage fighting in Britain. His CDs include *Survival of the Shittest* and *Genetically Modified... Just for You*. Mat is currently filming a 90-minute drama for BBC 2.

Chrissie Gittins

Chrissie Gittins has won prizes in the Lancaster Literature Festival Poetry Competition, *Poetry News* competitions, the Yorkshire Open and Ottakar's Faber Poetry Competition. Chrissie's poems have been widely anthologised, as well as printed in *the Observer, the Independent on Sunday, Reactions 3* and broadcast on BBC Radio. In 2003, Arc Publications published her first collection, *Armature*. Her radio play, *Starved for Love*, starred Patricia Routledge and Emma Cunniffe and was broadcast to wide acclaim on Radio 4 in 2002.

Martin Glynn

Martin Glynn has developed residencies and creative projects all over the world. An established Arts Development consultant, he has worked alongside many arts agencies in the UK and abroad. As a workshop facilitator he has a strong reputation for delivering arts-based programmes in areas such as youth and social work, prisons and probation, training, libraries and education.

Salena Saliva Godden

Salena Saliva Godden has been published in *IC3, Gargoyle* and *Oral*. She features on the recent Coldcut albums, *Let Us Play* and *Let Us Replay* (Ninja Tunes) and subsequently toured extensively in Japan and across Europe. In 1999, Salena co-created *Saltpetre*, a spoken word concept for CD and radio. Promoting and documenting the thriving spoken word scene, Saltpetre Radio enjoys a weekly slot on the UK's first independent art radio station, Resonance FM104.4.

Alexander D Great

In the mid-60s, Alexander D Great became a professional musician-songwriter, creating his own style from a mix of Beatles, blues and Baroque music. Alexander returned to his Trinidadian roots in the late '80s, creating *Socablues*, his own fusion of calypso, soul and blues. In 1998, Alexander wrote the first full-length calypso opera, Rumshop, staged at the Lyric Theatre, West London. He divides his time between his ten-piece band, running his own small record label and facilitating workshops in schools and colleges.

Emma Hammond

Emma Hammond's observational poetry focuses on character and story, weighing down delightful frivolity with a darker twist.

Choman Hardi

Choman Hardi has published two volumes of poetry in Kurdish, *Return with No Memory* and *Light of the Shadows*. She won the 2003 Jerwood-Arvon Young Poet's Apprenticeship and performed in the South Bank's Poetry International Festival 2002. For the British Council, she has travelled to Brussels, India and the Czech Republic. Bloodaxe will publish her first collection in English in 2004.

Karen Hayley

Karen Hayley has performed around Europe, and been featured on Channel 4, Sky, BBC Radio 3, at the Soho Writer's Festival, and is now very popular in Holland, for some reason. She now presents the MTV UK nighttime slot from nine till midnight, seven days a week. Karen has recently performed in the Rotterdam International Poetry Festival.

John Hegley

After *Glad to Wear Glasses* in 1990, John Hegley published another six titles, all filled with verse, prose, drawings, drama and photographs of potatoes, and the CD, *Saint and Blurry*. He has worked with two children's theatre groups, Interaction and Soapbox, and began his highly successful career at the notoriously tough Comedy Store in 1980. His first notable media exposure was the John Peel Sessions (Radio 1) with Popticians in 1983–4.

Hilaire

Born in Melbourne, Hilaire has lived in London since 1986. Her poetry has been published in many magazines and broadcast on Dutch and Australian radio. She performed with Apples & Snakes at the Edinburgh Fringe Festival, 1998. Her short stories have appeared in *5 Uneasy Pieces* (Pulp Faction), *The Ex Files* (Quartet), *Suspect Device* (Serpent's Tail), *Neonlit* (Quartet) and *Her Majesty* (Tindal St). Her novel *Hearts on Ice* was published by Serpent's Tail in 2000.

Kazuko Hohki

Kazuko Hohki came to England from Tokyo in 1978. In 1982 she founded the Japanese female pop performance group Frank Chickens, which had an independent chart hit with *We Are Ninja*, released five albums and toured worldwide. Kazuko has made solo albums and written several multimedia shows, including *My Husband is a Spaceman* and *Toothless*, which was chosen for *Time Out*'s Critics' Choice in the British Festival of Visual Theatre. She was a founding member of the Japanese American Toy Theatre of London.

Michael Horovitz

Michael Horovitz was an early champion of the oral and jazz-poetry scene whose flamboyant performances have energised audiences on both sides of the Atlantic. The Poetry Olympics Festivals, which he founded in 1980, have taken Horovitz all over the world. He performs a one-man-poetry-band show and also gives lecture-recitals featuring jazz-poetry recordings and slide projections of his Bop Art drawings, collages, picture-poems and jazzpaintry. He co-edited *New Departures*, as well as the *POW!* and *POP* anthologies.

Mahmood Jamal

Progressive Pakistani filmmaker, poet and translator Mahmood Jamal has been published in many anthologies; broadcast on radio and TV; contributed to the 3rd World Writer's Forum *Black Voices*; coordinated Troubador Poetry; co-edited *Black Phoenix*; edited and translated *The Penguin Book of Modern Urdu Poetry* (1986); won the Arts Council Award for translating poetry; and performed in major venues across Britain.

Mark Gwynne Jones

Mark Gwynne Jones is a poet whose work crosses over into physical theatre and the visual arts. An engaging and energetic performer, Mark has presented his work on a wide variety of platforms from Edinburgh to London.

Jackie Kay

Glaswegian Jackie Kay's first collection, *The Adoption Papers*, was awarded the 1992 Forward Prize. She has published two books of poetry for children, *Two's Company* and *The Frog Who Dreamed She Was an Opera Singer*, and written widely for stage and television. In 1998 her poetry collection, *Off Colour* (Bloodaxe, 1998), was shortlisted for the TS Eliot Prize. Her first novel, *Trumpet* (Picador, 1998), won *the Guardian* Fiction Prize and a Scottish Arts Council Book Award.

Fatimah Kelleher

Co-founder of the spoken word collective Urban Griots, Fatimah Kelleher has performed widely in England as well as abroad, including taking part in the 2001 City of Women Festival in Slovenia. She has worked as a teacher in Sudan, teaching English language and conducting poetry workshops.

Mimi Khalvati

Mimi Khalvati trained as an actor at Drama Centre London and worked as a theatre director in Iran and the UK. Her Carcanet collections include *Mirrorwork*, for which she received an Arts Council of England writer's award, *In White Ink*, *Entries on Light* and most recently, *The Chine*. Her *Selected Poems* was published in 2000 by Carcanet. She is founder and coordinator of the Poetry School and co-editor of the school's second anthology, *Entering the Tapestry* (Enitharmon, 2003).

Shamshad Khan

Shamshad Khan's poetry appears in anthologies such as *Flame*, *Poetry of Rebellion*, *Gargoyle*, *the Firepeople*, *Bittersweet*, *Healing Strategies for Women at War*, *Longman's GCSE Poems for Your Pocket* and Redbeck Press' collection of British South Asian poets. She has been featured on the Bradford Festival Radio, GMR and Radio 4's *Love Thang* and *Woman's Hour*. She has performed widely and is co-editor of an anthology of Black women's poetry (Crocus, 1999).

Mike Ladd

Mike Ladd received an MA in Poetry from Boston University. He has been published in many literary magazines and several anthologies, including *Aloud: Voices from the Nuyorican Poets Café*, *In Defense of Mumia*, *Bum Rush the Page*, *Por La Victoire* and *Everything but the Burden*. Michael has written and produced five albums, *Easy Listening For Armageddon*, *Live From Paris*, *Welcome to the After Future* and *The Infesticons: Gun Hill Road* and *The Majesticons: Beauty Party*.

Inge Elsa Laird

Born in Germany of Hungarian and Jewish ancestry, Inge Elsa Laird has lived in the UK since 1962. She has had translations of her minimalist poetry published in *the Financial Times*, *Jewish Chronicle*, *New Departures* and *Gargoyle*, among others. She was for many years co-editor of *New Departures* and co-organiser of the Poetry Olympics Festivals, and works as an interpreter and translator. Her book of poetry, *Poems*, was published in 2002 by the Elephant Press.

Fran Landesman

Fran Landesman arrived in London in 1964 and began a new career as a performing poet. She wrote the lyrics to *Spring Can Really Hang You Up the Most* and *The Ballad of the Sad Young Man*, which have been covered by Ella Fitzgerald, Sarah Vaughn, Chaka Khan, Barbra Streisand and Bette Midler. Having written songs with Dudley Moore and Alec Wilder, in 1994 she began collaborating with Simon Wallace and the duo has produced more than 150 songs.

Liz Lochhead

Poet and dramatist Liz Lochhead lectured in Fine Art for eight years before becoming a professional writer in the '70s. Since then, she's worked extensively in theatre and TV, including writing *Damages* for the BBC, and been widely published. Her books include *Dreaming of Frankenstein* and *Collected Poems* (Polygon, 1984), *True Confession* and *New Cliches* (Polygon, 1985), *Bagpipe Muzak* (Penguin, 1991) and *Mary Queen of Scots Got Her Head Chopped Off* (Penguin, 1987).

Jared Louche

American-born, London-based Jared Louche is a poet, musician, writer, teacher, entertainer and multimedia artist. His first book of poetry was *A Handbook on How to Wreck Other People's Lives* (Gut Punch Press) and his forthcoming book, *The City of Ondo*, is an ambitious collaborative multimedia project. Jared has recorded and performed extensively with his seminal machine-rock band Chemlab, whose new album, *Oxidizer*, is out in 2004 on Invisible Records.

Paul Lyalls

Paul Lyalls has performed at numerous Edinburgh Festivals and many prestigious venues from New York to Belfast. He has run hundreds of workshops in schools, youth projects and prisons. His children's show *Are We Very Nearly There Yet?* is currently touring. His published work includes the books *Are We Very Nearly There Yet?*, *Evolver* and the forthcoming *Samplified*, and the CD *Chill*.

Stacy Makishi

Stacy Makishi's solo show, *Tongue In Sheets*, toured the US and UK, and she has collaborated many times with the Obie Award-winning New York company Split Britches. She has enjoyed teaching residencies at Harvard, MIT, William & Mary College, Wellesley College, Rose Bruford and Queen Mary College, and received awards, fellowships and endowments, as well as commissions from CBS and FOX. Her recent work, *Eat More Spam*, was included in the International Film Festival in San Francisco. Her latest multimedia project is *Cinema Bizarre!* In 2002 she was part of Apples & Snakes' *Writers on the Storm* tour.

Aoife Mannix

Aoife Mannix's chapbook is *The Trick of Foreign Words* (Tall Lighthouse) and her first novel is due in 2004 from Xpress. In 2002, Aoife participated in the Apples & Snakes *Writers on the Storm* project. Her work has been anthologised in: *Short Fuse, The Book of Hope, In Our Own Words, 100 Poets Against the War, Gargoyle* and *Westside Stories* (Xpress) as well as numerous magazines. Aoife's poetry has been broadcast on BBC's Radio 4, London Live and World Service.

Roger McGough

Roger McGough is one of Britain's best-known poetry voices, with regular contributions to BBC Radio's *Booked, Poetry Please* and the World Service. His list of publications include *The Spotted Unicorn, Sporting Relations* and, for children, *Bed Bad Cats* and *Until I Met Mr Dudley*. Born in Liverpool, his numerous collections have established him as one of the most distinctive and powerful voices in contemporary poetry. Roger McGough has been awarded an OBE and The Cholmondeley Award for Poetry for his work.

Adrian Mitchell

Adrian Mitchell has given over a thousand poetry readings throughout Britain, Europe, USA, Africa and Asia. Adrian's works include, *The White Deer, The Wild Animal Song Contest, Mowgli's Jungle, The Snow Queen* and *The Pied Piper* for children and, for adults, *Tyger* (the National Theatre) and *Man Friday*. Adrian's version of *The Lion, the Witch and the Wardrobe* was premiered by the Royal Shakespeare Company, for whom he also adapted *Alice in Wonderland* and *Through the Looking Glass* for the stage. He has also written three Beatrix Potter plays which have been staged by the Unicorn Theatre for Children. He writes plays for television, lyrics for shows and adapts foreign plays for the theatre.

Mr Social Control

Mr Social Control has performed all around the UK. His poems have been appeared in magazines *Red Pepper, the New Humanist*, the anthology *Red Sky At Night*, on BBC Radio 4, Resonance FM and on his live CD *The War Against Abstract Nouns*. His first play, *No, It Was You*, opened in London in 2003.

Patrick Neate

Patrick Neate is a versatile writer, reluctant journalist, occasional scriptwriter and poet. His first novel, *Musungu Jim and the Great Chief Tuloko* (Penguin, 2000) won a Betty Trask Award, while his second, *Twelve Bar Blues* (Penguin, 2001) won the Whitbread Novel Prize. Since then, novel *The London Pigeon Wars* (Penguin, 2003) has been followed by the non-fiction *Where You're At: Notes from the Frontline of a Hip-Hop Planet* (Bloomsbury, 2003). His short stories have been broadcast on BBC Radio 4 and published in several anthologies and magazines. As a spoken work artist, Patrick has toured and taught around the UK.

Grace Nichols

Grace Nichols was born in Guyana in 1950 and has lived in the UK since 1977. Her first poetry collection, *I Is a Long-Memoried Woman*, (1983) won the Commonwealth Poetry Prize and a film adaptation won a gold medal at the International Film and Television Festival of New York. Subsequent poetry collections include *The Fat Black Woman's Poems, Lazy Thoughts of a Lazy Woman* and *Sunrise*. She also writes books for children, inspired predominantly by Guyanese folklore and Amerindian legends, including *Come on into My Tropical Garden, Give Yourself a Hug*, and *The Poet Cat*.

Bette O'Callaghan

Bette O'Callaghan has unexpectedly reached her 55th year. She performs regularly at poetry venues in London, has been published in *Rising* and other fanzines and has published chapbooks *Runnin' On Empty* and *Lipstick and Ammunition*. Her work is included on the inaugural spoken word CD, *Saltpetre*.

Owen O'Neill

Owen O'Neill is an established comedian, writer and actor. He made his TV debut on *Saturday Live* in 1985 and has since performed on numerous TV shows, including his own stand-up special for the BBC. He has performed worldwide, including gigs in Hong Kong, China, Melbourne, Frankfurt, Toronto, Los Angeles and Lisbon. He is a regular on the UK comedy circuit and has performed on *the David Letterman Show* and *the Conan O'Brien Show*.

Rachel Pantechnicon

Rachel Pantechnicon has been on the UK poetry scene since 1999. Before that, her appearances were confined to the Borough of Merton, which doesn't really count. Rachel enjoys reading poetry, writing poetry and meeting people in poetical situations. She writes mainly for her cat, Harold, but some of her work has been known to appeal to humans. Her story books for children include *Michelle in the House of Crisps* and the *Cheesegrater Leg-Iron Lion* series.

Brian Patten

Brian Patten's collections of poetry include *Love Poems* and *Armada*. His books of verse for children include *Gargling with Jelly* and *Juggling with Gerbils*. He is the author of the award-winning novel, *Mr Moon's Last Case* and has edited many anthologies, including *The Puffin Book of 20th Century Children's Verse*, as well as writing for radio, stage and television. His work has been published in and translated into many languages.

Chloe Poems

Frequent hits at the Edinburgh Festival, Chloe Poems' theatre shows, *Knockers*, *Chloe Poems' Healing Roadshow*, *Universal Rentboy*, *Kinky* and *ME*, have toured up and down the country, from Aberdeen to Portsmouth. A stalwart of the cabaret circuit, Chloe has performed and hosted a wide range of events, including Gay Pride. As Associate Artist in the Green Room, she has become a champion of the Manchester poetry scene with her regular poetry slam, Slam Bam Thank You Ma'am, and the UK's first performance cabaret slam, the New Bohemia.

Vanessa Richards

Vanessa Richards is a writer and performance artist from Vancouver, Canada, who relocated to London in 1992. She is founder and Joint Artistic Director for the multimedia performing arts company, MANNAFEST.

Michèle Roberts

Michèle Roberts was born in 1949 to a French mother and an English father and brought up in Edgware, North London. She studied at Oxford University and her published works include *A Piece of the Night*, *The Visitation* and *The Wild Girl*.

Roger Robinson

Roger Robinson was co-founder of Urban Poets Society and Chocolate Art and programmer of Apples & Snakes from 1997 to 2000. As a writer, he has performed at venues such as the ICA, Literature Forum, Barcelona University, Wordstock Festival and New Jersey Performance Arts Centre. In 2001 Lubin & Kleyner published his book of short fiction, *Adventures in 3D*. His one-man show, *The Shadow Boxer*, premiered at BAC in 2000, commissioned and developed by Apples & Snakes and Jericho Productions.

Michael Rosen

Born in Harrow in 1946, Michael Rosen's childhood ambition was to be a farmer or an actor (after weekly theatre visits). After a year at medical school, he studied English literature at Oxford and went on to write plays for the Royal Court Theatre and the BBC. His first poetry collection, *Mind Your Own Business*, was published in 1974. He's since written many successful volumes, including *Centrally Heated Knickers, Lunch Boxes Don't Fly, Michael Rosen's Book of Very Silly Poems, We're Going on a Bear Hunt* and a children's play, *Pinocchio in the Park*.

Jacob Ross

Jacob Ross is a poet, playwright, journalist, novelist, creative writing tutor and former editor of *Artrage Intercultural Arts* magazine. His first collection of short stories, *Song for Simone*, was published in 1986. In 2001 he toured his latest book, *A Way to Catch the Dust*, in Germany, Korea, Jordan, the Caribbean, West Africa and the Middle East, where he was Writer in Residence at the Darat Al Funun Arts Academy in Jordan. In 2000 the Peabody Trust commissioned him to run the Millennium Writers Master Class. He is finishing a novel, *The Season of the Souls*, and a new collection of short stories.

Joy Russell

Joy Russell's work has appeared in *Don't Ask Me Why: An Anthology of Short Stories by Black Women, The Fire People, IC3: The Penguin Book of New Black Writing in Britain*, and *Bluesprint: Black British Columbian Literature and Orature*. Born in Belize, Joy worked in London for many years as an assistant producer on TV documentaries such as *Pump Up the Volume, The Hip Hop Years* and *Rebel Music: The Bob Marley Story*. She lives in Vancouver and recently co-curated *Hogan's Alley Revisited*, an exhibition on Vancouver's forgotten black community.

Jacob Sam-La Rose

Jacob Sam-La Rose has performed at venues such as the URB Festival 2002, Bay Lit Festival 2002, Soho Theatre, Royal Festival Hall, Jazz Café and Victoria Theatre, Greece. His work has been published in *Osmosis, Bolz Magazine, Sable Literary Magazine, modern love* and *LSE Magazine*. He has facilitated workshops at the National Theatre, Arvon Foundation and Glyndebourne. He helps run Malika's Poetry Kitchen and maintains FYI, an arts events mailing list.

Kadija Sesay

Kadija Sesay is a literary activist, editor and publisher who has edited several anthologies of black writers' work and whose work has been published and broadcast in the USA, UK and Africa. Founder and managing editor of the litmag *Sable*, she has won several awards, including *Cosmopolitan* Woman of Achievement, *Candice Magazine* Woman of Achievement, *the Voice* Newspaper Award for Work in the Creative Arts and a Woman of the Millennium award.

John Siddique

John Siddique's work has appeared in anthologies such as *The Fire People, The British Anthology of South Asian Poetry, Kiss* and many others. In addition to chapbooks *The Devil's Lunchbox* and *UMMA*, he has made several records. He has appeared on BBC Radio 4, Radio 2, Granada TV and BBC TV.

Sharrif Simmons

Critically acclaimed performance artist Sharrif Simmons has been called this generation's answer to Amiri Baraka, Gil Scott Heron and the Lost Poets. Having toured throughout Europe with his poetry-funk-rock-world band, Black Monsoon, and recording with musicians March Cary and David Gilmore, Sharrif recently completed his much-anticipated CD, *Sharrif Simmons and the Black Monsoon*. He is published in the anthology *In Defensive of Mumia* and is currently working on children's fable, *Why Clouds Become Clouds*.

Lemn Sissay

Author of several collections of poetry, including *Morning Breaks in the Elevator* and *Rebel without Applause*, editor of *The Fire People: A Collection of Black British Poets* (all Canongate Books), and a performance pioneer, Lemn Sissay is one of the UK's foremost poets.

Cherry Smyth

Cherry Smyth is the author of *Queer Notions* (Scarlet Press, 1992) and *Damn Fine Art by New Lesbian Artists* (Cassell, 1996). Her work is included in *The Anchor Book of New Irish Writing* and she wrote the screenplay for the short film *Salvage*, which was later broadcast. Her debut poetry collection is *When the Lights Go Up* (Lagan Press, 2001).

Neil Sparkes

Neil Sparkes is a writer, visual artist and musician who has read and performed all over the world, from Cuba to Helsinki, from Israel to Australia. His two collections of poetry are *All Metal and Other Mens' Wives* and *Rumba Rumba* (both Hangman Books), and his work has appeared in many anthologies. As vocalist and percussionist of Temple of Sound, Neil has co-written and produced the albums *Peoples Colony No. 1*, *Shout At The Devil* and most recently *First Edition*.

Pauline Stewart

Pauline Stewart uses poetry and fiction writing to explore the concept of dialect, drawing on her own African-Caribbean background, her London upbringing and her experiences in Europe. She has written her own stage version of the children's tale, *The Pied Piper*.

SuAndi

Born of Nigerian and British heritage, SuAndi tours and lectures internationally. Her most recent ICA commission, *The Story of M*, received critical acclaim in both the UK and US. Her performances have included work on Channel 4 and three spoken word recordings, *Mother Country, Soliloquy* and *Homelands*. Her publications include *Nearly 40, Style, There Will Be No Tears* and *I Love the Blackness of My People*. She has public art commissions at the Lowry Centre, Manchester, and the Prom, Blackpool.

Steve Tasane
Winner of the Glastonbury 2000 Poetry Slam, Steve Tasane is as much at ease presenting popular poetry in schools or staging his shows at venues ranging from the Barbican to the 100 Club. His collections include *Bleeding Heart* (Gecko Press) and *Freakspeak*. He was programmer for Apples & Snakes from 1993 to 1997 and instigated Litpop poetry with his polyvocal poetry group Atomic Lip. He now co-hosts Pure Poetry, Soho Theatre's weekly poetry club.

Greg Tate
A cultural critic for *the Village Voice* and author of *Flyboy in the Buttermilk*, Greg Tate contributes regularly to publications such as *Rolling Stone, VIBE,* and *the New York Times*. In addition, he helped found the Black Rock Coalition, produced two albums on his own label, and composed a libretto that was performed at the Apollo Theatre. He lives in New York.

Thom the World Poet
Thom the World Poet has published hundreds of thousands of poetry broadsheets, 55 chapbooks, 3 CDs and 35 poetry and music improvisational tapes. Originally from Australia and currently residing in Texas, Thom has played a major role in the running of poetry festivals all over the world.

Leah Thorn
Leah Thorn has lead performance poetry workshops at venues such as Tate Modern and Tate Britain, the Imperial War Museum, the Tower of London, the Holocaust Survivors' Centre and the Maudsley Hospital. Her performances include the RSC's Tongues on Fire Festival; the Jewish Voices season at the Barbican; the Art of Disappearing, Prague; From Dark to Light, Budapest; the Aberystwyth International Poetry Festival; Raw Visions International Women's Theatre Festival, Cardiff; Amnesty International Youth Conference on Human Rights; Helikon Poets Cabaret, Tel Aviv; and Centre Dar Al-Nadwa, Bethlehem.

Christopher Twigg
Christopher Twigg's books include *Nature Poetry* (Knife Edge Press, 1992), *Adventures in the West* (TMG, 1994), *In the Choir* (Alces Press, 1997), which was Pick of the Week paperback in *the Guardian*, and *A Cherub That Sees Them* (Pollack Press). Christopher has performed at the Royal Festival Hall's Voice Box, on Channel 4 (as part of the LitPop series) and on BBC Radio 3's *Poetry 2000*. He is singer and guitarist for the neo-old-time urban hillbilly indoor rambler group Chicken of the Woods, whose eponymous CD is out on Floating World Records.

Curtis Walker
Award-winning performer Curtis Walker is known as The Don of Black comedy. Formerly half of the double act Curtis and Ishmael, he has toured across the world, as well as hosting the Leeds Carnival. One of the UK comedy circuit's most recognisable and respected acts, Curtis gives a personal view of where multi-cultural Britain is heading today.

Claire Williamson

Claire Williamson has published two volumes of poetry, *Blind Peeping* and *French Connections*. In 1996 she performed on the *Truth Is Optional* tour and is touring with *Words Allowed*. Claire lectures part-time at the University of Bristol on the Creative Writing for Therapeutic Purposes Certificate, delivering lectures and workshops at many universities on the subject. She organises and hosts poetry events, competitions and projects at Poetry Can and Bristol Poetry Slam.

Ann Ziety

Ann Ziety has performed throughout the UK and been involved in many theatre productions on the London fringe, writing, directing and acting in her own plays, working under her real name, Wendy Metcalf. Her children's poetry collection is *Bumwigs & Earbelles & Other Unspeakable Delights*. She teaches acting at Morley College and theatre studies at London Metropolitan University. She served as Apples & Snakes' first education officer, 1991–1993.